Bob Dylan

Bob Dylan

Like a Complete Unknown

David Yaffe

Yale UNIVERSITY PRESS

New Haven and London

The author acknowledges The College of Arts and Sciences at Syracuse University for its generous support of his research and the production of this book.

Yale University Press books may be purchased in quantity for educational, business, or promotional use. For information, please e-mail sales.press@yale.edu (U.S. office) or sales@yaleup.co.uk (U.K. office).

Set in Janson type by Integrated Publishing Solutions, Grand Rapids, Michigan.
Printed in the United States of America by Thomson-Shore, Dexter, Michigan.

Library of Congress Control Number: 2011920627
ISBN 978-0-300-12457-6 (hardcover : alk. paper)

A catalogue record for this book is available from the British Library.

This paper meets the requirements of ANSI/NISO Z39.48–1992 (Permanence of Paper).

10 9 8 7 6 5 4 3 2 1

ICONS OF AMERICA
Mark Crispin Miller, *Series Editor*

Icons of America is a series of short works written by leading scholars, critics, and writers, each of whom tells a new and innovative story about American history and culture through the lens of a single iconic individual, event, object, or cultural phenomenon.

For Amy, and for Julian

And every one of them words rang true
And glowed like burnin' coal
Pourin' off of every page
Like it was written in my soul from me to you

Contents

Contents

Acknowledgments

The journey of writing, not writing, and writing this book again has taken me to some unexpected places, an astonishing range of the joys and sorrows life can bring. Fortunately, the joys have prevailed, and I thank every person and every institution that helped me arrive where I am now. Thinking about Bob Dylan began to seem necessary when I was fifteen. Making sense of my ideas, and trudging beyond a crowded field of exegetes, really took being twice that age, toward the end of a first book and realizing I had been sitting on the next one for years. I knew I was in for a terminal case when I was no longer obsessing over just *Blonde on Blonde* or *Blood on the Tracks* but also *Infidels* or *Oh Mercy*. Listing everyone who ever contributed to my thinking on Dylan would require some sort of repressed memory therapy.

There are certain individuals that stand out, though. Elon Green provided counsel on the playlist; Steve Elworth, Jim Hoberman, Jonathan Rosenbaum, and Jim Morrison (not that one, the other one) gave wise advice on the film chapter; Morris Dickstein paved the way for thinking of Dylan in a broad cultural context; and David Hajdu set high standards for music and culture writing and has been a cherished and supportive friend. Dan Torday continues to be a wonderfully supportive friend as well as an excellent guitar player, singer, and literary interlocutor. The University of Minnesota, Twin Cities; the CUNY Graduate Center; The New School; and Columbia University invited me for lectures that bore fruit in these pages. At Minnesota, I met Kevin Dettmar, who had already commissioned my essay for the *Cambridge Companion to Bob Dylan*, and who became a wonderful colleague and confidant. I also profited from conversations with John Barner, who, with Thom Swiss, commissioned another Dylan essay for the University of Minnesota Press. I am grateful for the permission to reprint passages in altered form. I also thank Alex Kafka at the *Chronicle of Higher Education*, Adam Shatz, formerly at *The Nation*, and Michael Agger at *Slate*, who each edited my pieces on Dylan (for Michael, there were three!) and who gave me space to set my sails. I am also grateful to John Palettella, my astute and generous editor at *The Nation*, for giving me a free hand, granting me time off from my music critic duties to complete these pages, and welcoming me back when I was ready.

I have had the good fortune to be gainfully employed at Syracuse University, where I have taught Dylan, and where I have made some lasting friendships and enjoyed writerly camaraderie among colleagues. Harvey Teres has been a brother to me in many ways (he will know what this means) and was among the first people here to make me feel at home. I am also grateful to many other colleagues, past and present, including Johanna Keller, Chris Kennedy, George Saunders, Brooks Haxton, Bruce Smith, Dana Spiotta, Silvio Torres-Saillant, Peter Mortenson, Dympna Callaghan, Arthur Flowers, Michael Burkard, Mary Karr, Sandy Sternlicht, Kevin Morrison, Ken Frieden, Scott Lyons, Stephanie Shirilan, and Mary Gaitskill. Gregg Lambert and Erin Mackie both supported me in their capacities as

English department chairs, and I thank the university for a paid semester's sabbatical. I am also grateful to anyone else who gave me kindness and splashes of jocularity or showed an interest in my work. I am grateful to Gerry Greenberg, Senior Associate Dean for Humanities (among many other duties), who graciously and assiduously helped with accessing the university's subvention fund for production costs. I also spent the 2008–09 school year as the Gould Faculty Fellow at Claremont McKenna College, where I was brought out by the formidable Bob Faggen, and where I got to enjoy stimulating intellectual relationships with a West Coast posse that included Bob, Adam Bradley, and Keri Walsh. Kevin Dettmar was steps away at Pomona, also a boon.

Many other friends were tremendously supportive and loyal, including Jeff Cassvan, who generously treats me like family, putting me up in NYC again and again, Krin Gabbard, John Matteson, Jessica Firger, Garret Keizer, Ansel Elkins, Joe Hooper, and Severin Garanzuay. These simpatico souls are always there for me, and I for them.

I also thank Eric Lott and Mark Crispin Miller for, quite simply, making this possible. My indefatigable agent Chris Calhoun has provided me with fervid advocacy and sage counsel. It has been an honor and a pleasure to write this for Yale University Press. I thank Jonathan Brent for signing me up with immense enthusiasm and for providing early editorial feedback. Bill Frucht, who took over, turned out to be everything this writer could possibly want. He knew how to ask a single question that could generate an entire chapter in a matter of weeks. Call it editorial transference or mind reading, it was truly rewarding to work with him. Jaya Chatterjee was more than just an excellent editorial assistant. I highly valued her intelligence, insight, and ideas, along with her professionalism and patience. Jack Borrebach dutifully handled the production, Joyce Ippolito assiduously midwifed the copy, and Linda Webster crafted an index that was a road map to this book's soul. I thank Jeff Rosen for his generous permission to reprint Dylan's lyrics, and Geralyn Huxley at the Andy Warhol Museum for assisting with permissions and production for the frontispiece. I also thank Sarah Crichton at FSG for her investment in me and her saintly patience.

Thanks to my parents, not Dylan fans but fans of mine, who gave me life more than once, and who continue to give me joy, support, and love. And the biggest thanks of all—really, "thanks" seems such a small and insufficient word—is for my wife, Amy Leal. Amy Leal, Amy Leal, Amy Leal, repeat until full, printer. She is wise, she is passionate, she is intuitive, she is funny, she is beautiful, and I thank my stars that she is mine. I love her too much for an acknowledgments page to even accommodate. When we met, she was a Paul person and I was a John person. I became more of a Paul person and she became more of a Bob person, with a love that speaks like silence. She has shared my passions and understood my mind and soul and has given us our son Julian, who already loves music, and who I hope will grow up to enjoy these pages. This book is for them.

Introduction

Another Side

In 2007, Bob Dylan, for the first time, was ready to be remixed. In the world of rock and roll, it was as if Leonardo da Vinci were giving his blessing for Marcel Duchamp to draw his Mona Lisa moustache. At the turntables, and arranging the ska horns, was Mark Ronson, who had worked with Macy Gray, Amy Winehouse, and Lily Allen, among others. The producer was, in other words, a millennial hipster, and he retranslated a 1966 track from *Blonde on Blonde*, "Most Likely You Go Your Way (And I'll Go Mine)," into a re-vamped language, augmented by a group called the Dap-Kings. Fortunately, there was nothing defacing about the results. The drums were changed, brass was added, and levels were altered to imagine a Dylan song on a dance floor for these new, insufferable kids. Director Rupert Jones filmed the entire video in Williamsburg, Brooklyn, the epicenter of the moment's urban hip (a neighborhood so precious, "cool hunters" from various marketing groups take the L train to check it out). Open casting was announced in search of various Dylan look-alikes, just from behind, and it was no shock that the hood was full of wannabe Dylans. Jones did not miss a single detail. To accompany a track barely longer than three and a half minutes, we follow the back of Dylan's head through nearly half a century. We begin with a Super 8 image of Freewheelin' Dylan with a Suze Rotolo look-alike on his arm (bypassing a man with twenty pounds of headlines stapled to his chest), then they enter a car, but Dylan comes out alone, now in black and white, ready to toss the "Subterranean Homesick Blues" placards. He keeps moving, leaving behind a crashed motorcycle, changing into cowboy boots, and black and white becomes color. He does not miss "Lay, Lady, Lay" opportunities in an urban Woodstock, but he does not hang around, either. Eventually, he is moved by the image of a black gospel choir perched on tenement steps and then a group of young black breakdancers strutting in front of a barbed wire fence decorated with graffiti. He enters a club, sees people dancing to this version of his music, but does not participate. He walks out into the night, wearing a cowboy hat and the kind of Western garb he has sported at recent concerts. Soldiers from Iraq whiz by. Night falls as he walks by the Williamsburg Bridge, guitar case in hand. We do not know what is coming next. The song is over.

Writing about Bob Dylan in the first decade of the twenty-first century is like that video, as if recalling a series of dreams. Millennial Dylan gives us truly eccentric interpretations of himself (*Masked and Anonymous* in 2003, *Chronicles, Vol. 1* in 2004) and gives license to Mark Ronson and director Todd Haynes (*I'm Not There*, 2007) to go for broke. Dylan does not see his own history as linear, and he seems to interpret himself more thematically than chronologically. In fact, he overlaps, looking back, forward, then back again. Thus, his astonishing memoir *Chronicles, Vol. 1* starts in 1961, jumps to 1970, then 1987, then reverberates back to 1961, deliberately skipping the most crucial moments (perhaps saved for a future volume, perhaps not). Thus he allows his career to be summed up in a short video that nevertheless hit the right points for a brief and vivacious summation. This book is in the spirit of these interpretations. Each chapter is thematic, not historical, even though the chapters, separately, move chronologically. When you finish a chapter in the twenty-first century, you will begin the next one back in the 1960s. What happened? There is another theme to cover. The themes include Dylan and singing, Dylan and blackness, Dylan and film, and Dylan and plagiarism. Together they attempt to elucidate the difficult pleasure that is Dylan, with his nasal voice, oblique lyrics, complicated relation to race, and controversial appropriation of words and music. Yet Dylan stays forever young, except that with each rebirth, he is also forever uncanny. This is a song of Dylan's selves. Dylan contains multitudes, and a book attempting to get to his genius must examine both the Napoleon in rags and the complete unknown, the Jokerman and the Queen of Spades, the lover and the thief. Taken together, they respond to what Dylan is giving us now, and the ways he is engaging our responses. You go to a Dylan concert in the twenty-first century—and in each year of the first decade, he played around 100 concerts, sometimes as many as 113—and you are either frustrated that the songs don't sound the way they do on the record (uninitiated) or are fascinated by the change (initiated). There are the Bob Cats, the Dylan equivalents of the Grateful Dead's Deadheads. They live for heading for another joint, and many people live for far less. Anything spontaneous or altered is adored, scrutinized, perhaps tweeted. How many songs on guitar and how many on keyboard? Did he smile? Did he make a stray remark? Did he croon or did he bark? What did he add to the mythology?

Indeed, if anything has been constant in Dylan's career, it's change. He walks into the car as one guy and exits as someone else. "I'm not there, I'm gone," he sang, and yet here he is, sort of. As Richard Gere says on the voiceover toward the end of *I'm Not There*, "Me? I can change during the course of a day. When I wake I'm one person, when I go to sleep I know for certain I'm somebody else. I don't know who I am most of the time." Now, Dylan's change is part of what his diehard fans appreciate. Many of Dylan's younger fans don't necessarily care about the 1960s and don't care if he's Jewish or Christian or either. The songs and the singer just speak to them. We live in a moment when we no longer want to attack the old Dylan for leaving us, or for imagining that any change is permanent. It's all part of the record now, but the longer he stays on that never-ending tour, he will also continue on an always changing cultural experiment. Go to a Dylan concert today and you will be prepared for what he will do, but not exactly how he will do it. You have an idea he will play around fifteen songs and two or three encores. It is likely that a new song or two will find a place alongside well-worn chestnuts like "Visions of Johanna," "I'll Be Your Baby Tonight," or "Tombstone Blues," and "Like a Rolling Stone" and "All Along the Watchtower" will be in the encore. Sometimes he'll throw in something he has never performed before, like "Billy." Sometimes he'll dust off a song he hasn't played for years, like "New Morning." You can be sure there are plenty of people keeping track, sending the setlists to be archived on the website expectingrain.com (an allusion to a phrase from "Desolation Row": "Everybody is either making love or else expecting rain"). You may feel transformed; you may feel disappointed. He may feel the same way. But he reinvents his past to the point where it becomes his future. "The future to me is already a thing of the past," he sang later in life, when he could be whimsical about it all.

This book is for people who want to revisit Dylan's past in the present tense, for mongrel dogs who teach, writers and critics who prophesize with their pen, mothers and fathers throughout the land, and everyone else who cares or is just curious. Why have we been making a such a big deal about Bob Dylan for half a century? Does he illuminate us or confuse us, or both? Does he seduce us or repel us? Sing sweetly or nastily? Is he the master breakup artist, or does he want us to bring that bottle over here? Bob Dylan is all of these things and more. He exists on stage and in our dreams, our fantasies, our real and concocted histories, our colleges, our state fairs, and our concert halls at the same time. He is a text, yet he is still a moving target, unwilling to be pinned down. He exists as history, and yet he lives, walking into that dark, foggy unknown. This book will marvel at an accumulated half-century while continuing to ponder what can never be answered. "How many roads must a man walk down before you can call him a man?" Dylan asked when he was just getting started. This book does not pretend to have an answer. More important is getting a handle on the man who asked the question, in all his assumed identities. The roads are still worth the hike.

ONE

The Cawing, Derisive Voice

"I am just as good a singer as Caruso. Have you ever heard me sing? I happen to be just as good as him. A good singer. You have to listen closely. But I hit all those notes and I can hold my breath three times as long if I want to." This is sheer bravado from the twenty-three-year-old Dylan of *Dont Look Back*, but he also has a point. It's true that he could never match, note for note, the bombastic and virtuosic thrill of hearing Enrico Caruso. Nor—need it be added?—did he have the technique. What he could match was intensity, but his was of a kind no one had quite heard before. This was a moment when Dylan had never been more obnoxious or inspired, a time when almost everything he said, including the Caruso remark, needed to be taken with a healthy dose of irony. In 1965 he made both *Bringing It All Back Home* and *Highway 61 Revisited* in a frenzied rush of brilliance and venom. Philip Larkin—an English poet with an ambiguous relationship to American music—memorably described Dylan's "cawing, derisive voice," and he provisionally meant it as a compliment.[1]

The biggest misconception about Dylan, among the unbelievers, is that his cawing derision is somehow an impediment to appreciation. The second biggest (and this is among the believers) is that he is a poet before he is a lyricist and a performer, and that the latter two represent a demotion of the first. It seems reasonable to call Dylan a poet if he is placed next to his mentor Allen Ginsberg, but to place him next to the sublime John Ashbery, Elizabeth Bishop, James Merrill, or—why not?—Frank O'Hara, Robert Lowell, Wallace Stevens, or T. S. Eliot (despite, or maybe because of, Dylan's reference in "Desolation Row" to Pound and Eliot "fighting in the captain's tower") is to commit an act of aesthetic anachronism that does Dylan and much of the *Norton Anthology of Poetry* a disservice.

Dylan's influences seem to emanate from all over: Arthur Rimbaud here, Walt Whitman and Elvis there, Cisco, Sonny Bono, an' Leadbelly too. Yet it's hard to know where, precisely, to place him. Put him in the Great American Songbook with George and Ira Gershwin, Cole Porter, Irving Berlin, Harold Arlen, Duke Ellington and Billy Strayhorn, and the rest and the fit isn't quite right, either; the flat-picked chords are too simple, not like changes to be played.[2] Dylan staked out a cultural space that was well trodden, but in a combination unlike anyone else's. As he put it in the spoken-word intro to "Bob Dylan's Blues" (1963), "Unlike most of the songs nowadays that are being written uptown in Tin Pan Alley— That's where most of the folk songs come from nowadays—This, this is a song, this wasn't written up there. This was written somewhere down in the United States." Dylan is delivering a zinger: the idea of "folk songs" written in Tin Pan Alley is ridiculous; folk songs are supposed to be rural, anonymous, and communal—a righteous public domain with no royalties. When Dylan cast himself as being "somewhere down in the United States," he wasn't talking about geography. "Some people, they tell me, I have the blood of the land in my voice," Dylan would sing in 2009, a kind of Steinbeckian self-mythologizing with a wink and a nudge. But if Dylan was just another regular guy, he would have never written "Yonder stands your orphan with his gun" or any of the other gnomics with which he confronted his listeners in 1965. Whether those listeners were high or sober, his lines were unfathomable, yet at the same time seemed to make sense. Dylan belongs in the canon of singer-songwriters—a category he practically invented in the modern era of song. In the 1960s he was a new kind of hybrid, and it took his inimitable brand of articulation, more familiar to conversations than songs, to get it across. What could be annoying in conversation—adenoidal stream-of-consciousness vitriol—could be addictive when set to music.

Those Tin Pan Alley songwriters that he wasn't quite of—Jews, outsiders, Negroes, homosexuals (not all of whom literally worked in Manhattan's Flower District "Tin Pan Alley" offices but, lyrically and musically, occupied a Tin Pan Alley of the mind)—all strived for sophistication in a vernacular mode. When Dylan sang Gershwin's "Soon" in a tux for a 1987 television special, it sounded as if Tom Joad had shown up at the Algonquin Round Table. Dylan came out of a much different tradition from that of those prewar urban tunesmiths, those who feasted on the Alan Lomax field recordings that brought black geniuses toiling in the Jim Crow South to the record players of middle-class towns like Hibbing, Minnesota. Dylan was shaped by the cult of authenticity that venerated some of his favorites—Muddy Waters (an inspiration for the title of "Like a Rolling Stone"), Odetta (who inspired young Dylan to pick up acoustic guitar), and above all Woody Guthrie, who inspired the prophetic lines of Dylan's first major song: "Hey, Woody Guthrie, I wrote you a song." "Hey" is not exactly a sophisticated form of address, but it is intimate and heartfelt. It echoed the sort of thing Guthrie himself wrote when he was addressing a land made for him and us. It is a form of address that has emerged out of the fields and into the corridors of power. Half a century later, "Hey" is more accepted than it was in 1961, especially in cyberspace, where it has all but replaced "Dear." When it comes to something as malleable as sophistication, the center cannot hold.

While Dylan avoided sophistication in favor of authenticity, sophistication had a way of finding him. This is clear not only in what he would write by the time he made his Caruso claim, but by the heavy reading he was clearly doing in the incubation period recounted in *Chronicles, Vol. 1*. Joyce, Ovid, Proust, Keats—nothing major seemed to escape him. That derisive caw had elements of poetry and a schmear of the Great American Songbook. And so, while he is perhaps miscategorized as a poet, he is underrated as a singer. The two go together. Even though the unconverted thought Dylan's brilliant lyrics needed sweeter voices to reach to the top of the singles charts (Peter, Paul, and Mary; Stevie Wonder; the Byrds), to get their full power you needed that caw. Without it, no Leonard Cohen, no Lou Reed, no Patti Smith, no punk rock, no grunge. The entire persona of Bruce Springsteen would have to be reinvented from scratch. Neil Young would be unthinkable. Lucinda Williams said, "I really decided to learn how to write great songs because of what I considered my vocal limitations. I decided I was going to be the female Bob Dylan."[3] Even Jimi Hendrix, who famously covered a few Dylan songs, said the man helped give him the confidence to sing. The *vox mirabulus* of 1965 forced listeners to confront what Ralph Waldo Emerson meant when he advised his readers to "go upright and vital and speak the rude truth in all ways." Leonard Cohen, upon first hearing *Bringing It All Back Home* and *Highway 61 Revisited*, declared that he would become the new Bob Dylan, when he already had three books of poetry, a novel, and a national bad boy reputation under his belt but had never sung a note in public (Nadel, 142). Perhaps the talking blues of "Subterranean Homesick Blues" even prepared the world for guttural hip-hop. Dylan didn't invent all the things he was doing, but he consolidated, assimilated, and with that relentless voice became one of the most influential forces in American Song.

And yet the voice on *The Freewheelin' Bob Dylan* (1963)—and its follow-up, *The Times They Are a-Changin'* (1964)—was probably its least original feature, steeped as it was in Dust Bowl affections and Woody Guthrie worship. The songs were thrilling and built to last: "Masters of War," "Girl from the North Country," "A Hard Rain's a-Gonna Fall," "The Lonesome Death of Hattie Carroll," and of course, the song that would forever transfigure the way we would comprehend air and velocity, "Blowin' in the Wind." Yet for all his scruffy, boyish appeal, his voice sounded like it wanted to be older than it was—closer to the ancient croak it would become by the new millennium. You might say he was young and unlearned, but he had to sacrifice Woody. The next chapter of Dylan emerged on *Another Side of Bob Dylan* (1964) but really came into its own when he put a gerund into a title without dropping the *g*: From the ashes of "freewheelin'" and "changin'" came *Bringing It All Back Home*. And just as the *g* in *Bringing* was intact, so it was in the voice. In a song that Dylan allegedly liked, David Bowie famously described his sound as a "voice like sand and glue," but the Dylan sound of 1965 was shocking for its clarity.[4] Many years later, Dylan would be heard, on less articulate nights, as a swami making you an offer you couldn't understand. But in 1965, contrary to the canard, you could understand every burning word.

Dylan's wholly distinctive, original voice—a "thin, wild mercury sound," to use a phrase of his coinage—emerged from the ashes of his career as a political pamphleteerer. The shift in diction came after he scandalized the National Emergency Civil Liberties Committee by accepting an award and drunkenly saying, just weeks after the assassination of John F. Kennedy, that he identified with Lee Harvey Oswald. The event was a catalyst for Dylan to abandon his "finger-pointin'" songs (until the 1970s, when the stories of George

Jackson and Hurricane Carter pulled him back in) to look inward. In one of the innocuous statements he made early in this near-career-sinking speech—Dylan's equivalent of Malcolm X's "chickens coming home to roost" comment—he tried to age backward: "I want to thank you for the Tom Paine award on behalf of everybody that went down to Cuba. First of all because they're all young and it's took me a long time to get young and now I consider myself young. And I'm proud of it. I'm proud that I'm young." Before the moment that became the most memorable part of the speech, he went on, in the face of the geriatric crowd, to praise "everything leading to youngness." This was a decade before he would intone "And may you stay forever young" but shortly before he recorded "I was so much older then, I'm younger than that now." Those Dust Bowl ballads he was writing to perfection were prized for authenticity, a quality that, in his milieu, was more important than Tin Pan Alley sophistication. (Even though performing in Oakieface was no less a mask than, say, Ella Fitzgerald or Billie Holiday singing Cole Porter to perfection, drenched in Porter's New Haven–honed wit.) But Dylan becoming young was another kind of authenticity: he was only twenty-two years old. Getting young meant, for Dylan at the close of 1963, getting real.

And by the time 1964 was under way, Dylan, out of the Dust Bowl and into the city, found an entirely new disguise: himself, or at least another side. At a concert on October 31, 1964, at Lincoln Center's recently opened Philharmonic Hall (later renamed Avery Fisher), Dylan, no longer dropping his *g*'s, commented on his ever-changing personae: "It's just Halloween. I've got my Bob Dylan mask on [applause, laughter] . . . I'm masquerading." That was the year that Dylan gave the Beatles their first taste of marijuana, when his romance with Joan Baez peaked out but only Dylan realized it, and also a year of two albums, one *The Times They Are a-Changin'* (February), featuring an identity already bypassed with the most thrilling collection of "finger pointin'" songs he would ever produce, and *Another Side of Bob Dylan* (May), less earnest, more playful, and almost completely apolitical (save a reference to "equality in school" in "My Back Pages," and "Chimes of Freedom," droned in a nearly anesthetized haze), a demonstration that he was not merely presenting another side but had shape-shifted, in just a few months, into something almost entirely different. Sex, drugs, and irony replaced politics and earnestness. It was a tradeoff that, for a young pop star with taboos to tweak, was pretty hard to resist.

Dylan's transformation from political sloganeer (or "protest singer," a term he would come to loathe) to surreal, fragmented, Beat-influenced songwriter has generated rivers of ink. What is less remarked on is how this shift (on record, in a matter of months) changed his singing. Even though Dylan made a defiant move against the topical, in many ways his phrasing, his attack, his pronunciation, his speak-song changed what it could mean to be a popular singer, especially one with literary ambitions, and it changed the way one sang (or spoke) American without tears.[5] Between 1964 and 1966, as Dylan's voice went from Guthrieite to big-city shouter to drugged-out gnomic adenoidal seer, the whole world, as he sang, was watchin', or listenin'. The voice would continue to evolve in subsequent years, but its metamorphosis (much to Dylan's relief) would no longer be a barometer of cultural change. Freaks would still dig through his garbage and regard him as a reluctant prophet. He would still claw his way in for comeback after comeback, no matter how much he wanted to be left alone. And he performed far more concerts in the first decade of the twenty-first century than he did during the 1960s.

So much attention has been paid to the electric shock at Newport and the birth pangs of Dylan's rock stardom—accompanied by a chorus of boos everywhere he plugged in back in 1965 and 1966— that it threatens to dwarf the equally seismic shock of his acoustic music of that period and the startlingly new voice that it featured. It wasn't booed, but that didn't mean his acoustic self was not unleashing something more subtly heretical. The folknik cry of "Judas"—said the Englishman to the Jew—was such a circus, partly because indignant listeners could not understand the words under the sweet, nasty riffs emanating from Robbie Robertson's guitar. But if they really were listening, they might have wanted to get a rope anyway. "And if my thought-dreams could be seen / They'd probably put my head in a guillotine." These are the closing words of the acoustic masterpiece "It's Alright, Ma (I'm Only Bleeding)." The song was first belted out at his 1964 Halloween concert at Lincoln Center, where every cascading image he spit out was met with rapt confusion. This was some kind of a protest song, perhaps against reality. And it was sung not at all like a folk song. The guitar beat out a repeated blues riff, but there was no attempt to emulate blues diction. The lyrics were allusion after allusion, beginning with a shout-out to Arthur Koestler ("Darkness at the edge of noon") followed by a seemingly random splattering that would make it into Bartlett's ("But even the president of the United States / Sometimes must have / To stand naked"—a follow-up to Allen Ginsberg's question to America, "When will you take off your clothes?") and a line cited by Al Gore as his favorite quotation when he was running for president and answering a question by Oprah: "He who is not busy being born is busy dying." That derisive caw was the sound of a new life, a new character that flouted notions of folk singing, pop singing, even polite conversation. These were bad words spewed out by a bad boy, and the mind that brought them to life was the same one that snarled and lashed the words. Anyone listening to Dylan in 1965 did so by flashes of lightning. That caw generated the storm.

An outtake from the notorious *Dont Look Back* scene where Dylan shows up Donovan is a perfect example of how even his croons could be deadly. In the spring of 1965, Donovan was touted throughout Dylan's English tour as the flavor of the month—the first of the "new Dylans," some of whom offered far greater quality. The new Dylans always had some similarity to their original (for Donovan, who would improve later, it must have been the hair) and would usually pay as much respect to their original as Dylan had paid to Woody. In his two-song performance before a small room of nervous cigarette smokers (including the recipient of the command performance, a twitchy, chain-smoking Donovan) Dylan plays a caustic "It's All Over Now Baby Blue" (which, in part, makes it into *Dont Look Back*) and a lyrical "Love Minus Zero/No Limit" (which doesn't, but is now on the DVD extras and YouTube). "Baby Blue" is all scorched earth, as if every eviscerating syllable could get Donovan off his territory. "Love Minus Zero" is achingly tender; Dylan is nothing like his pretender, sitting trapped and terrified a few yards away, and even further from parody. He emphasizes the lines that only he could come up with ("The *wind* howls like a *hammer*," perhaps a nod to Minnesota winters, a mixed metaphor that somehow blends in the context of the entrancing strum, and of the words that come next). He isn't adenoidal, whiny, or incoherent, but he is carefully intoning as delicate a love song as he would ever write. His guitar is somewhat out of tune (a frequent habit—in the name of authenticity or carelessness), but each syllable packs a punch, each vowel makes a point, and the meaning—perhaps difficult to take in when it was still so new—is nevertheless available to the knowing listener.

If Dylan wasn't trying to show up Donovan, he was avenging himself on every other turncoat, fraud, or phony that stood in his way. What was he looking for when he romanced Warhol Factory floozie Edie Sedgwick? Someone to discuss Chekhov with? (The woman who could discuss Chekhov would have it no easier.) Warhol introduced them, sort of. (A match made in the Factory! This would surely last.) Plus she was a beautiful, blond model and a drug addict. The relationship, needless to say, did not endure, but the songs it inspired certainly would, including "Like a Rolling Stone," "Leopard Skin Pillbox Hat," and "Just Like a Woman." Their story is a familiar one of celebrity skin, but the voice it brought out in him was something else altogether. After he cut his teeth on the civil rights movement and causes that ran from the global (the military-industrial complex inspiring "Masters of War") to the satirical, and from the banned ("Talking John Birch Paranoid Blues") to the obscure (the also unreleased "Who Killed Davey Moore," not knowing exactly where to point his finger in search for justice in a boxer's death), his finger was still pointing, at those who crossed him or even disappointed him, and, of course, as he gained perspective, pointing the finger at himself would be the most devastating critique of all. Dylan in 1965 was, as a singer, never more naked.

He would find distractions in Columbia's Studio A, where out-of-tune pianos were deliberately used to create a saloon aura, and where few musicians seemed to bother to tune their guitars. (The virtuoso blues guitarist Mike Bloomfield, playing blistering licks, was the exception.) Even Tom Wilson, after producing "Like a Rolling Stone," was shown the door because he had the temerity to point out that Al Kooper, who played organ on the record, was not an organ player. Dylan didn't want anyone telling him who was or was not an organ player. (The record, amateur organ and all, went to number two and is now a classic rock shrine on perpetual replay, so what did Wilson know?) Needless to say, no one in those days told him how to sing, either. If it was a blues number with an allegory vaguely inspired by *Moby-Dick*, Dylan would dig deep into Howlin' Wolf and Herman Melville, emerging a blues-based obsessive literature reader on amphetamines and brilliance. The mind is ever present in the voice, should anyone wish for a mellifluous cover. If he's bidding adieu to Edie Sedgwick, he sounds wounded, tough, and oddly vulnerable. "You break just like a little girl," he spouts, but he sounds like he's falling apart himself. On paper, it's too mean. On record, it's tender, even self-lacerating. The voice could howl like a hammer and break like a little girl.

The freedom of Dylan's sung speech between 1964 and 1966 was no accident. Certain people were waiting for a *Howl* that could also rock, a Woody Guthrie on mescaline and Rimbaud. The rage emanating from Mario Savio, the leader of the Free Speech Movement on the steps of the University of California at Berkeley's Sproul Plaza at the end of 1964, was unintentionally getting the world ready for Dylan going electric—though not, it turned out, fast enough. During his most famous speech, the police dragged Savio away just as he was getting started, as they did with Lenny Bruce around the same time. (The latter inspired a 1981 song by Dylan, who recast Dirty Lenny as Christlike Lenny.) In 1966 Mike Nichols's adaptation of Edward Albee's *Who's Afraid of Virginia Woolf* scandalized the censors, besotted the critics, won five Oscars, and helped kill the morally restrictive Hays Code in Hollywood. Dylan, unlike Bruce or Albee's Martha, was not one to curse in public. Nor was he, like Savio, one to fulminate about conspiracy theories, at least not in speech. But he was one to raise his voice, make it nasty (not sexually but sonically), and make public displays of adenoidal vitriol an accepted form of public entertainment. Even though the police never intervened, the folk police made their dissent clear.

The rest of the Dylan persona underwent radical revision along with the singing. The Dylan of *Dont Look Back* was cheeky, irreverent, sometimes hostile (to the clueless *Time* magazine interviewer who inspired Mister Jones in "Ballad of a Thin Man"), but always lucid, even if he'd had a sip or a puff. The Dylan of 1966—and when we speak of his public persona of that year, we are referring only to the first half, before his mythic motorcycle crash—was zonked out, droning, on another planet. *Dont Look Back* seemed like relative innocence to *Eat the Document*'s shaky experience. And yet he was still in creative overdrive, in some ways more than before. *Blonde on Blonde* demanded two discs, and one of its songs, "Sad Eyed Lady of the Lowlands," took up an entire side. He recorded verse after verse with Nashville studio musicians, who had no idea what the hell he was singing about ("My warehouse eyes / My Arabian drums") or why he kept adding verses but gave him the sound he needed. On record, he hit the notes when he felt like it, and when he didn't, it wasn't incompetence but spontaneity. As Ginsberg was trying to sing, Dylan was, in a musical way, trying to talk. "Where are you tonight sweet Marie?" he asked on a single that went nowhere. The drawn out long *u* on "you" would become the sort of thing people would parody, even with affection. "Rainy Day Women # 12 and 35" remained a crowd pleaser decades after it was recorded, but it was the equation between toking up and a public stoning that made it Dylanesque. He sounded intentionally stoned while singing it. (This is your Dylan on drugs.) When he revisited it four decades later in concert, he sang it more like a grizzled bluesman than a druggie. But in 1966, his pharmacological intake inflected his singing. The caw became a drone.

"He had a face like a mask," sang Dylan in 1989. A self like a mask? A sound like a mask? Even though he was singing about The Man With the Long Black Coat, he could have just as easily been singing about himself in any given period. Sometimes, though, the mask was more pronounced. The mask could be the performance, or sometimes the thing the mask is covering is the performance. On his 1966 European tour, Dylan would get booed in the electric section with the Hawks and draw rapt attention for the solo set. As throughout his career, he would have on and off nights. "Visions of Johanna," a then-unreleased gem that Dylan was unearthing on the solo sets, would get naked emotion when he could deliver it, and adenoidal mannerisms when he couldn't. But when there was no barrier between himself and the audience, as on the version recorded May 26, 1966, available on *Biograph*, he really does sound like he's been "up past the dawn." On the high notes ("to play *tricks* when you're *trying* to be so *quiet*") each peak is a plea made with what Keats called full-throated ease, although there was nothing easy about the material or the performance. Other nights, including the "Royal Albert Hall" concert (actually recorded in Manchester's Free Trade Hall on May 17)—Dylan used nasal mannerisms to replace anything too vulnerable. Sometimes, being up past the dawn means having not enough performance energy. The voice could be a mask or an open wound.

Between the two "Visions of Johanna" performances, on the night of March 17, 1966, the most notorious heckler in rock-and-roll history called Dylan "Judas!" It might have gone the other way, no matter who was getting paid. Most people agree that it was Dylan who was deceived by his hostile fans. Much of the indifferent singing—on the nights that it was indifferent, including much of the acoustic portion at Free Trade Hall—was surely for their benefit, a sonic "fuck you" that was all the more naked with the acoustic instrumentation they obviously preferred. He didn't think they were worth the more tender emotions and gave them calculated artifice. "I wish I could get me a new Bob Dylan so I could *use him*," he complained one night backstage in England. Whether he was complaining about his inability to give it his all against the hecklers, or whether he was feeling a need for change, he got it in July of that year, when he may or may not have fallen off that motorcycle badly enough to cancel his plans—including a television special—for the rest of the year. The singer who emerged on the songs from Big Pink in Woodstock in New York—a few of which appeared in 1975, on a belated album titled *The Basement Tapes*, but the majority of which were heard only in other peoples' mouths or on some of the most hallowed and circulated demos in rock history—is notable for his lack of conscious affect. He took his sidemen from that breakneck 1966 jaunt, along with their rightful drummer Levon Helm, who had no stomach for the booing and bailed on the European tour, and recorded demos never meant for public consumption. A rock critic's 1997 paean, Greil Marcus's *Old, Weird America*, showed how much hunger there was from the genre of writing Dylan arguably inspired as much as anyone—even the Beatles—and how appetizing it was to plumb the famously private artist's subconscious, particularly at such a hermetic moment. Dylan thought Marcus overstated the case; he was re-creating not the world of Harry Smith 78s but his actual experiences of encounters with some of the musicians on those records back in his busking days. Dylan would never be more intimately heartfelt than on "Tears of Rage," cowritten with Band keyboardist Richard Manuel, where he reaches notes he hadn't hit on earlier recordings or records. He's not singing in his speaking voice, but he's not singing in a calculated voice, either. He's playful, laidback, sometimes a little soused. He's also ignoring the Summer of Love and its fallout. At one point, when a member of The Band put on the newly released *Sgt. Pepper,* Dylan, who had forged an alliance with the Beatles, retorted: "Turn that shit off."

Within a year or so, George Harrison would visit Dylan and The Band at Big Pink, and it was clear that his Beatles alliance remained. The impulse was not to shut down the Beatles, but to shut down the Summer of Love and all the psychedelic dandyism that went with it. (Does he contradict himself? He wanted to join the Grateful Dead a couple of decades later, with or without tie-dye.) Dylan was living in Woodstock, New York, in 1967, and it seemed as far from hippie counterculture as you could get: never mind that his mere presence eventually attracted half a million hippies to a festival named for the town (though the festival itself took place in a different town), and even The Band was on the bill. But just when the world was ready to accept the electric Dylan—the crowd at Monterey Pop who cheered Jimi Hendrix burning his guitar and wailing on it with his teeth would surely have accepted the electric din from Dylan's 1966 tour—he turned inward, some said backward. Greil Marcus argues that the Dylan of the *Basement Tapes* period went back to those Harry Smith 78s. Dylan's "I Shall Be Released," his own "Midnight Special," was a song about redeemed prisoners, and Dylan was clearly listening to a lot of gospel music, if his "People Get Ready" cover is any indication. The basement is about as far as you could get from the stage, and Dylan was incubating. Robbie Robertson might have written "Stage Fright" about himself or about Dylan, but Dylan clearly sounded as unaffected as he would ever be. Of the songs that were part of the *Basement Tapes*, The Band ended up recording "Tears of Rage" and "I Shall Be Released," Nina Simone—one of Dylan's most soulful exegetes—also covered "I Shall Be Released," and Manfred Mann covered "Quinn the Eskimo" with an English accent. The tapes achieved an aura, false starts, multiple takes, and even bad jokes ("See You Later Allen Ginsberg"). Dylan's was a voice that suddenly could croon, hit the lower notes with authority and the higher ones without nasal strain. This was the Dylan that didn't exist in public.

His first trip out of hibernation, on January 20, 1968, accompanied by The Band, was for a memorial benefit concert for Woody Guthrie, who had finally succumbed to Huntington's disease the previous October. In the afternoon set, Dylan belted out blistering performances of Guthrie's "I Ain't Got No Home," "Dear Mrs. Roosevelt," and "Grand Coulee Dam." Even though the band rocked as hard as ever, the mere sight of Dylan holding an acoustic guitar—it might have said "This Machine Kills Critics"—evoked nostalgia, not a favorite emotion for Dylan. Especially on "Grand Coulee Dam," he sounded nothing like his *Basement Tapes* incarnation— more like he was summoning the dead. "Grand Coulee Dam" is actually a pro-government song, celebrating one of FDR's most cherished public works projects. But Dylan sounds like he's neither shilling nor undermining. He is celebrating the man who beckoned him to New York, to another self, a man whose guitar killed fascists (while Dylan's electric one couldn't silence angry folkies). Dylan was twenty-six but sounded like he had already lived many lives, traveled many roads. Edward Albee wrote in *The Zoo Story,* "Sometimes you have to go a long way out of your way to come back a short distance correctly." Dylan went a long way to come back to this incarnation of Woody. He had come to Carnegie Hall not to imitate him but to channel him with the self he happened to be at that moment, not at all the green folkie who had set the world ablaze just a few years earlier. This was *Basement Tapes* Dylan with The Band, except that once the adrenaline of the moment came to the surface, he pushed those songs out with all his might. The year would continue to slouch toward Bethlehem. That afternoon, in broad daylight for all to see, Dylan was soaring to Woody. It was the first electric performance where he was not booed.

"A Voice Without Restraint"

By 1968, Dylan's voice was no longer that of his generation, no matter how much that generation nipped at his heels. It would continue to evolve, hitting various peaks and valleys and peaks again. It would try on new things, like sincerity. It would also test out the decibel meter at the well-oiled rock concert when he went back on tour, in 1974, and find that the meter was endless. He could howl as loudly as he wanted, and the cheers would keep coming. That tour with The Band lasted for only a couple of months, and he must have acted like a rock star backstage—perhaps egged on by those bad boys playing with him—in ways that destroyed his marriage and altered his being. Religion, some great writing, and various forms of cultural anachronism followed. Comebacks were whispered about until the big one came and never quite left. His voice kept changing, settled for a while, then changed some more. Joan Baez came back into the fold when Dylan's marriage was breaking up on the 1975–76 Rolling Thunder Revue, and she even came back for a couple of stints: a 1982 concert for peace and a 1984 tour with Carlos Santana for nothing more noble than money and art. She was the only singer who truly knew how to follow Dylan's every capricious move; she chose politics and he chose the muse, and its sound would follow the ravages of age, along with more ravaging substances, even those legal killers that can really do damage to the larynx: cigarettes. Dylan kept aging like everyone else, but people noticed a whole lot more because he was not everyone else.

On *John Wesley Harding*, released at the tail end of 1967, Dylan made a respectable showing with critics and record buyers but found a new way of saying *go away*. Since listeners were hearing *Basement Tapes* tracks only underground, this new album could not have made a starker contrast with his last official album, *Blonde on Blonde* and the rattled performances of 1966. By the time *John Wesley Harding* was released in 1968, the hostile youth had found a more satisfying outlet than booing at a Dylan concert. The inclusive utopia of civil rights would splinter that year into the separatist baiting of "Black Power," when assassins' bullets would kill Martin Luther King, Jr., and another Kennedy, when the Tet Offensive inspired dodgings, burnings, Yippies, hippies, Up Against the Wall Motherfuckers, and a radical group whose name was lifted from a Dylan line: Weatherman. Dylan didn't need one to know which way the wind blew. He had a television; he knew what was going on. In 2004 he finally shared his perspective of 1968—mostly as a bewildered private citizen and a parent—in *Chronicles, Vol. 1*. Of the hippies who were repeatedly breaking into his house, he said, "I wanted to set fire to these people." Even as *John Wesley Harding* commenced a period when Dylan would sing of prophets ("I Dreamed I Saw St. Augustine") and folk heroes ("John Wesley Harding"), he was also, quite deliberately, no longer prophetic; he was a calculated anachronism. He describes St. Augustine as having a "voice without restraint," and maybe he was unshackling his own, having gone from folk to rock to something else—call it acoustic homiletics. "I pity the poor immigrant," he drones, invoking those striving Italians, Irish, and Jews who landed on America's shores at the beginning of the twentieth century and wondering if they should have made a round trip. The vocal is morose, almost a parody of self-righteous leftist guilt, a far cry from the up-tempo version he performed with Joan Baez in 1976. Dylan is somewhere in the wilderness of pre-Woodstock Woodstock, surrounded by a growing brood, dabbling in painting, thumbing through the Bible, singing about landlords, tenants, businessman winos; he mischievously rhymed "moon," "June," and "spoon" on an infectious country number that turned out to be a classic but that was delightfully archaic, whimsical, and sincere, all the things he wasn't supposed to be. One of the songs, "All Along the Watchtower," would be turned into an anthem of 1968 by no less a musical trailblazer than Jimi Hendrix and would eventually become Dylan's own most performed song, done in the Jimi style. But at the time he sounded, at all of twenty-six, too old, or perhaps too mature, to be a magpie anymore. He sounded more like a preservationist, a labor historian, a minimalist. His icons were no longer of this earth. As Woody lay dying, Dylan was preparing a new way to live, or at least to dodge, crooning his way to a séance, far, far away from the apocalyptic days of 1968, a moment that summoned what Philip Roth called the "American berserk."

In 1966, the "Judas" crowd wanted Dylan to sound like 1963. In 1969, they wanted him to be like he was in 1966. They didn't understand that he was the way he was partly because it *wasn't* what they wanted to hear; they weren't prepared for it. It took producer Rick Rubin and an aging Johnny Cash to make country music cool for young people, beginning with Cash's *American Recording* (1994), made the year Kurt Cobain committed suicide and collegiate hipsters—many of whom, like Cash, were already clad in black—found "alt country." But in 1969, hipster country would have been a contradiction in terms, perhaps even a sellout. Dylan's voice underwent its most dramatic transformation that year, hitting the lower frequencies, part Hank Williams, part Pee-Wee Herman. In a head-scratching interview with *Rolling Stone* editor Jann Wenner, he claimed he got his new voice from kicking cigarettes. Even though the man with the newly golden voice seemed miles away from his *Dont Look Back* incarnation, the idea of a changing voice brought him back to that old provocation to *Time* magazine: "I tell you, you stop smoking those cigarettes [laughter] . . . and you'll be able to sing like Caruso."

Dylan was laughing because he knew he was not singing like Caruso. But he had also eschewed bratty whining for retro baritone masculinity. He cut his hair and was already apparently getting prepared for his role as Alias in *Pat Garret and Billy the Kid*. Elvis's baritone resounded in the mid- to late 1950s, but the Beatles, the Beach Boys, and all their imitators sang like choir boys. Mick Jagger intoned Howlin' Wolf as a bad boy (as opposed to man) and Dylan's mid-1960s voice sounded like a college kid on amphetamines arguing about ontology. He was now at the other side of his twenties, he had gone to Minnesota to bury his father in 1967, and when he came back to Woodstock, where he was prepared to be a one-man vigilante to protect his family from longhair intruders until common sense prevailed, Dylan was not the dazzling magician of *Blonde on Blonde*. Instead, he seemed to be entering, in a countrified Old Testament–prophet way, some version of manhood. He was the elegist, on "I Threw It All Away," who lamented losing the breastlike mountains in the palm of his hand, a lover who would command his woman to "Lay, Lady, Lay" (a hit single and nearly the opening song of "Midnight Cowboy"), and a sexual rambler who would assure his two-night-stand gal, "Tonight, I'll Be Staying Here With You."

Singing duets with Johnny Cash made him some new fans and baffled some of his old ones, who would associate that music with the same crackers Dylan was pointing fingers at in the halcyon days of 1963. Dylan cared about as much as he did when people gasped that another hero, Pete Seeger, was a Communist. Cash had already given Dylan his guitar at the Newport Folk Festival, leaving him weak-kneed. The 1969 duet of Dylan's 1963 "Girl from the North Country" with Cash, when it aired on the *Johnny Cash Show*, is like hearing, or watching, masculinity as mimesis, where Cash is the former and Dylan the latter. Dylan is twitchy, looking around skittishly while reinventing his old lines into an older voice. Cash sings Dylan's words like he owns them. Dylan would later say that Cash was like a "God-like" figure to him, a musical patriarch after he had lost his real one. Their sessions, a rag-and-bone affair, were widely bootlegged. It would be many years before Dylan would go back there again. He picked up smoking again and was reunited with his adenoids.

Dylan didn't make it back to the lower reaches of his voice until he lost control and then blew out his upper range. He had some wild times before he came crashing down, only to find, eventually, that if down was good enough for Cash, it was good enough for him. For some reason—vanity, hanging on to youth, indifference—he held on to those uncomfortable notes until what once was drama became decay, and it took a while before he realized what decay could do for him, that it could be, if handled right, something divine. Dylan the howler emerged on *Planet Waves* (1974), his first number-one album, a hastily cobbled reunion with The Band that found him testing his voice out for bigger, larger, and unsubtle; this was an album that had two versions of "Forever Young" as well as a song rhyming "crotch" with "watch." Rock and roll had become big business during the eight years that Dylan had played house. He prepared himself to play stadiums and arenas—venues that had mainly been reserved for sports events. This was a long way from the Gaslight, Newport, or even Free Trade Hall. Everyone would be able to hear him, he could crank up the volume and wail to his heart's content, and he would hear nary a boo among the thousands. Dylan must have been daunted. *These people worship me. How can I unsettle them?* He couldn't. This would initiate the period—one that had no end—in which Dylan, having nothing else to revolt against, defiantly raged against the melody. "Most Likely You Go Your Way (And I'll Go Mine)" was venomous enough on *Blonde on Blonde*, but he poured salt on the wound by refusing to even resolve the melody. Instead, his voice would keep reaching for the heights, ending every line—"mine!!"—with vituperative throat gargling. It must have been cathartic. With new melodies came new emotions. They were all breaking the sound barrier. Where were the boos, emanating from nostalgists who missed the melodies? Critics were receiving him like a hero or a god. Everyone was giddily blathering that Dylan was back. He never sounded so furious.

"You Can Always Lose a Little More"

The story of Bob Dylan's voice from the mid-1970s to the first decade of the twenty-first century is less a story about an evolving nation and more about Dylan busy being born again and again. *Blood on the Tracks* (1975), despite its imagery of surveillance and paranoia, had nothing to do with Watergate and everything to do with a dismantling marriage and an exposed soul. The album was first recorded and nearly released based entirely on New York sessions, with a melancholic Dylan accompanied only by a bass guitar and occasional organ. At the last minute, he revised lyrics and rerecorded some tracks with a local band in Minnesota. The released album was a hybrid—pity and rage. On the Minnesota tracks, with their higher keys, Dylan sings out of his comfort zone, which in turn provides objective correlative. But it also got him into bad habits. The Minnesota sessions were anthems of revenge, laceration, and the kind of yelling that must have been happening while his marriage dissolved. (Jakob Dylan would later say that he couldn't listen to the album because it sounded like his parents fighting.) While Minnesota was more withering, New York was more raw, more vulnerable, cast as a lyrical elegy.

There was no way Dylan could transfer something so personal, so revealing, to live audiences, or duplication of any kind. (The closest was an impromptu never-released performance of "Abandoned Love" at the Other End in 1975. Such intimacy was harder to reproduce on the larger stage, or even in the studio. *Blood on the Tracks*, particularly the New York sessions, is an Aeolian harp of sorrow. Forget about therapy. These are more like catharsis incarnate. "It's a wonder we can even feed ourselves," he mopes at the end of the New York "Idiot Wind," snarls at the end of the released Minnesota version, and screams at the end of the live performance released as *Hard Rain* (1976). Dylan went from morose to livid in little more than a year. He was never so blatant as when he sang of staying up all night in the Chelsea Hotel writing "Sad Eyed Lady of the Lowlands" for Sara, his "radiant jewel" and "mystical wife." It made no difference. Dylan was laying himself bare to get the love of his life back, and it got him nowhere. Such *weltschmerz* was not easy. His voice could inspire millions without moving the one listener he needed most.

Sara continued to haunt the more emotionally raw songs on *Street-Legal* (1978), especially the last and most desperate cry of all, "Where Are You Tonight? (Journey Through Dark Heat)," in which he is amazed by his survival but disappointed by his solitude. Then, of course, Robert Zimmerman became a Christian, of the holy-roller and Bible-thumping variety. To those who opposed his collaboration with Johnny Cash and wanted a secular humanist as a rock star avatar, it was the ultimate betrayal. For Dylan, this must have been gratifying. The singer on *Slow Train Coming* (1979) is not markedly different from the singer on *Street-Legal*, but the singer on *Saved* (1980) is. *Saved* was recorded after Dylan had completed a tour in which he refused to play anything but *Slow Train Coming*, when he started getting boos for an entirely different reason. It was Judas all over again. By the time he recorded *Saved*, he was writing songs with gospel changes, immersed in the diction of his African American backup singers. He sounded so intensely taken with his new identity, it was hard to believe that he got disillusioned so soon after. *Shot of Love* (1981) is half a Christian album (what a half, especially the Blakean "Every Grain of Sand"), and Dylan, still sonically gospelized, is pushing his voice further than it should be pushed. His response is to keep pushing, and before the end of the 1980s, he will have lost an octave.

"When you think that you lost everything / You find out you can always lose a little more," he sang in 1997. The art of losing, says Elizabeth Bishop, isn't hard to master. It's not so easy to experience, either, and listening to Dylan in the three decades that followed *Saved* is to witness, bit by bit, how he could still summon his greatest powers, not only *while* he was losing range in his voice but *because* of it. He made the thousand natural shocks his whole generation was heir to part of his art. He would sing about suffering while sounding like he had suffered. This was like the blues, but not exactly. This was not mere imitation of blues masters but a hybrid; the voice contained not only everything he absorbed, but everything he was. We followed Dylan's deterioration not only as an aesthetic phenomenon but as the narrative arc of a strange and mangled life, where the lyricism emerges when you least expect it. And what started out a strident whine became an increasingly pleasing croak, raspy croon, or graveyard-shift low-down and dirty blues. It is all too convenient to dismiss Dylan's 1980s as an awkward period of overproduction and strained vocals—when he was still trying to nail the upper-register notes he scorched in the 1970s. It is Dylan's least appreciated period, especially, based on interviews and comments in *Chronicles, Vol. 1*, by himself. The craft was still there if he wanted it, though, and the singing was no less emotive or authentic at its best. The *Basement Tapes* phenomenon continued: the majesties of *Infidels* (1983) could be most fully appreciated with what he kept off, and while the album contains dazzling songwriting and impassioned vocals, what he cut—like the jettisoned New York sessions of *Blood on the Tracks*—was so subtle and revealing, those who first heard them became convinced that Dylan was either losing touch with his best work or perversely keeping it in the hands of lo-fi bootleggers.

The album's obvious masterpiece, "Blind Willie McTell," was left off completely. On the demo that surfaced on *The Bootleg Series, Vol. 1* (1991), Dylan is unguarded in his tragic performance of racial appropriation and artistic aspiration. On a widely bootlegged rehearsal, in which he laughs over his first line, the private musical foreplay overshadows the main event. That rehearsal performance could have been—should have been—among his finest vocal performances. The tapes were officially released, and Dylan was repeatedly strident. Chilled out and holding back on the demo, he sounded fearless. Like an actor peaking at dress rehearsal, Dylan's musical concepts of 1983–84 were often most pleasing to the ear just before showtime. His rehearsals for the noir masterpiece "Sweetheart Like You" also surpassed the final version, most notably when he played possum in the lower regions of his middle-aged range; the lower notes actually sounded better. Dylan thought that he could be most dramatic, most Dylanesque, if he still hit the highest notes he could, without considering (or perhaps not caring) that the highest notes were also the least melodic.[6] In 1984, he appeared on *Late Night with David Letterman* and gave a powerful live performance, reconceiving "Jokerman" as punk rock. But the rehearsal was even better. Dylan's voice was supple and authoritative on the blues standard "I Once Knew a Man." The intensity meter on "Jokerman" was a little less frenetic and less strained. This was the period when Dylan's best singing was held back in private, and those who heard it got a bootlegged preview of what the 1990s did for him.

Dylan kept releasing albums throughout the 1980s, and even the most dismissed among them still contained privileged moments. Dylan was starting to sound like a parody of himself on "We Are the World," and on rehearsal footage—where, again, he sounded better than his completed take—with Stevie Wonder on piano, we can see Quincy Jones encouraging almost precisely the sound he delivered on the record. In July 1985, on one of the most-watched live television events up to that time, Dylan is distracted by the musicians setting up behind him for the finale, and the indecipherable Ron Wood and Keith Richards are not much help; he tries to sing in earnest but just gives up, shooting random notes into the Philadelphia sky. But in addition to coming up with the idea for the hugely successful Farm Aid right on stage, he was still able to be at his best when he was so inspired. The 1986 song "Brownsville Girl," cowritten with Sam Shepard, was a high point in a low period. It was a hybrid of a Shepard monologue and Dylan song, eleven minutes of trying to return to the past while realizing that it is not only inaccessible but mythical. This just makes him want to get back to what Robert Polito called Dylan's "memory palace."[7] In a particularly prophetic move, it begins with speech, lower than the notes he usually aimed for in 1986. As the song builds, the speech turns into singing, goaded by his backup singers, a paean to movies, music, and memory. Fantasy and myth won the day but could not forestall reality for long. Dylan was forty-five years old, packing in crowds in concerts with Tom Petty, but feeling spent as a songwriter and sounding jaded as a singer. This song happens to be a magisterial commentary *about* feeling spent. The subject is a conflation of Shepard's and Dylan's memories, and the performance is a desperate cry to remember youth and get it right, or at least to get it wrong in a poetic way. Life and its opacities intervene, and Dylan knows that moving forward through the fog can have a sublimity of its own. He yearns to get back to the place before "the stars were torn down." Which Gregory Peck movie was it? Which woman? He's not sure. (It's *The Gunfighter.*) He just remembers the feeling. Anyway, the stars only appeared to be real. They were an invention, like his voice. He would soon get a new one.

He came up with his latter-day persona while recording the Daniel Lanois–produced *Oh Mercy* (1989), which was not greeted as a major event in the music industry despite the kind of "comeback" *Rolling Stone* review that came around every few years. Dylan devoted an entire section in *Chronicles, Vol. 1* to the making of *Oh Mercy*, and even though he goes play-by-play and track-by-track and has many wry comments, he does not spend much space on the dramatic change in his voice. He left an entire register behind and allowed himself, at forty-seven, to sound older than he was. The drama would no longer come from his straining to hit the highest note but from following this character who had been so destroyed that everything was broken. As if he were actually aging—prematurely—into the character Tom Waits had been playing all those years, Dylan's rasp was its own kind of grain in the voice. Where had this wise man been hiding? Suddenly a wheeze could communicate as much as a shout—maybe more. In *Chronicles, Vol. 1*, Dylan describes how, before he wrote the lyrics for the *Oh Mercy* songs, he was recovering from a serious arm injury and recalling advice from the blues musician Lonnie Johnson on what sounded (implausibly) like a mathematical system for refreshing your vocal chops. Simply put, Dylan has always been impatient with melodies. In the rush of live performance, he had the tendency to go up. Now he was more likely to modulate down. Live performances from the late 1980s and beyond do not always back up the view in *Chronicles*, but the studio recordings did, and this was only one of the reasons *Oh Mercy* was a watershed.

This was the beginning of an era (which, like his tour, never ended) in which Dylan consciously avoided keeping up with the times but simply created his own. Even though choosing producer Daniel Lanois, at the suggestion of Bono, might have seemed au courant, the sound was an airy blues, as swampy as the Victorian New Orleans mansion-turned-recording studio where summer faded slowly into autumn; the city's musical traditions were blissfully stuck in the humid atmosphere. As he did in 1964, Dylan could return to an idiom closer to his speaking voice, with all the rasp and affect it had gathered over the years, the wear and tear from the twenty-five years he had spent being "Bob Dylan." Earlier in the decade, he sounded jaded and passive. The Dylan of 1985–86 was whining for help; let the producers inflict their studio hoodoo on this half-written song and let me outta here! But he couldn't run away from himself. "Brownsville Girl" is the sound of someone who could find his way back with a new magic. And *Oh Mercy* sustained that magic, in a different way. Even when certain songs weren't quite up to par ("What Good Am I?" "Disease of Conceit"), his new voice nailed every take. He was good at being old. He sounded like he could do it forever.

And so, it seems, he has. Dylan's next album, *Under the Red Sky* (1990), was not well received, despite some songs that would age well in concert (the title track, "God Knows," "Born in Time," "Cat's in the Well") and an official bootleg, but he used that same down-and-dirty voice that also made his outings with the Traveling Wilburys such a hoot. He recorded two traditional folk albums—

Good as I Been to You (1993) and *World Gone Wrong* (1995)—that contained material he could have used when he was starting out, but that had a gravity he could only have pulled off as the aging sage of Folkways; he is so visceral when singing of blood in his eyes that the condition sounds medical. Dylan spent the next seven years playing a truly death-defying number of concerts. In 1995, he played 116 shows. In 1996, eighty-six. In 1997, the year he "nearly went to meet Elvis" while getting treated for a rare heart infection called histoplasmosis, he still played a grueling ninety-four. Undaunted, in 1998 he played 110. This kind of schedule under less than ideal physical conditions would put a rasp in anyone's voice, and indeed Dylan's added even more rocks and gravel to the mix. Many thought he was done with songwriting for good, but *Time Out of Mind* (1997) was the comeback of all comebacks, with Lanois and his rootsy tool-kits and bar-band virtuosi back in the mix (with jazz genius Brian Blade on the drums holding steady and holding back). The whole thing was a tale from the crypt, but what a tale, and what a teller. This guy who can't seem to clear his throat sure has some tales of heartbreak to unload, along with self-doubt and self-reflection. He has lived the blues he sings, yet his heart, battered and bruised, still aches. "Every nerve in my body is so vacant and numb," he intones. "I can't even remember what it was I came here to get away from." In the 1980s, being jaded meant shrugging off a record. In the 1990s it was source material. There are so many ways to go down; every part of this malaise is a muse.

Dylan listeners in the new millennium have heard the voice take even more hits, and they see the guitar playing, perhaps weakened by arthritis or carpal tunnel syndrome, mostly sidelined for a little electric rhythm and a lot of hunched-over keyboard. He got as dec-orated as an old rock star could get: Grammy Awards for *Time Out of Mind*, a Pulitzer for an accumulation of work, an Oscar for "Things Have Changed" (2000), which he seems to carry with him

at every concert, a National Book Award nomination for his astonishing memoir *Chronicles, Vol. 1* (2004), and a National Medal of the
Arts from the White House (2010). All the while, he kept up his rate
of performances and also kept making albums: the remarkable *Love
and Theft* (2001), which proved he didn't need Lanois to shake out a
masterpiece, *Modern Times* (2006) and *Together Through Life* (2009),
both of which hit number one. *Modern Times* reached back to earlier
styles, where he crooned like a phlegmatic Bing Crosby; it also contained perhaps his greatest journey-through-the-valley-of-death
song, "Ain't Talkin." When that voice is brought down to a near
whisper, it sounds like it can tell tales from the other side, wherever
that is. *Christmas in the Heart* (2009)—with all profits to charity—
was not a morbid little Christmas but a stab at wheezing sincerity, at
its best with the polka "Must Be Santa," in which he sounded like a
contemporary of St. Nick. Dylan was Teflon at this point; he could
shill for Victoria's Secret without ultimately losing cred. He could
sing anything and get away with it, and that was in many ways a
beautiful thing. During the aughts, after another momentary musical phenomenon, *American Idol*, featured the music of Paul McCartney, there was a question about whether Dylan, one of McCartney's
few living peers, might also be featured—not such a leap considering that judge Randy Jackson played bass on *Under the Red Sky*. But
fellow judge and producer Simon Cowell would have none of it. He
said that Dylan's music "bores him to tears" and that "the Bob
Dylans of this world would not make *American Idol* a better show."[8]
Of course they wouldn't. Cowell's idea of a good singer is a bad
Stevie Wonder imitator, a Whitney Houston without real emotions.

And yet there was a place in the crumbling music business for
Dylan—a decade of two number-one records for an artist past sixty-
five, a feat no one has matched. Beyond industry success, Dylan has
a huge group of exegetes who will hang on to every word. If it is a
word from the past, then they will hang on with particular interest

in his intonation, his tone, his feeling, and even which key it's in. Unlike most rock audiences, who just want a human jukebox, people still show up at casinos, state fairs, and concert halls to hear how radical this new Dylan is, even if he seems to be doing a lot of grunting and barking. Dylan used to be pitted against new Dylans like Bruce Springsteen. Now the new Dylan is the old one. No one expects the voice of *Highway 61* or *Blonde on Blonde* or *Blood on the Tracks* any more. That voice is long gone. It is preserved on stacks of vinyl, reams of digital detritus, lost forgotten years, buried feelings, abandoned love. And as long as time will permit, an old man, past threescore years and ten yet still called Bob Dylan, will continue to sing, recasting those anthems in the voice he has at that moment. He will not be the old him. He'll be the new old him. One day, and we shudder to think of it, that self will be gone, too, filed alongside a voice at times more youthful and dangerous, at others more ecstatic with belief or ravaged by doubt: a cawing, derisive voice, forever taunting, forever seducing, forever finger-pointing, forever bitter, forever elegiac, forever panting, and forever young.

TWO

Screen Test

The Many Dylans of the New Millennium

In the summer of 1965, Bob Dylan paid a visit to Andy Warhol's Factory to sit reluctantly for one of Warhol's Screen Tests. This was already something of a ritual for the well known, a silent hazing, a consensual violation by celluloid. Between 1964 and 1966, Warhol would act as an amateur Cecil B. DeMille, testing out various figures not for an actual film but for a life in images, to be scrutinized sometimes violently, unfairly, in the worst of faith. But it was only a test. All the stars had to do was to sit down and do nothing, although the Tests showed, as a study in human behavior as much as a document of moving portraiture, that doing nothing was impossible. Luminaries from Susan Sontag to Allen Ginsberg, not known for their shyness, were unsure how to appear in a realm without words. Salvador Dalí was left without a canvas. John Ashbery appeared immobilized without his verse. All Lou Reed could do was drink a bottle of Coke, more as product placement for the Warhol silkscreen than for the soda.

In that hazy, crazy summer of 1965, when "Like a Rolling Stone" hit number two on the pop charts and Dylan was driven out of Newport by a pack of philistines posing as bohemians, Dylan, no doubt motivated by Edie Sedgwick's empty yet alluring visage, became perhaps Warhol's ideal subject. An exhibitionist only on stage, Dylan knew the camera loved him, but at that moment he did not love it back. If Dylan were making a movie about Dylan, it would be nothing like this. And yet there he is. See the man with the stage fright, or perhaps, already, the stage ennui. He is twenty-four, and there is nothing anyone can do about it. Close up, you can still see his little boy cheeks and puppy dog eyes. He looks like he could fall asleep. He has an itch and decides to scratch it. *Shrug.* Being Bob Dylan has apparently already gotten old. His bloodshot eyes stare into the lens like a mug shot, as if to say, "Look out, kid," or perhaps, "What was it you wanted?"

Many lifetimes later, in 2000, Dylan finally had a chance to see his story told as one that contained multitudes. He had become notorious for wielding control of his image and was apparently waiting for someone to realize that one was not enough. So he agreed to be represented as a woman in Dylan drag, a black boy, an aging cowboy, a variation on Rimbaud, a misogynistic actor, and even, for a segment that was cut, a little Chaplinesque tramp. All these identities were in the one-page treatment for Todd Haynes's *I'm Not There* (2007), a film that would—in a premise counterintuitive to Hollywood orthodoxy—actually *celebrate* the impossibility of pinning down Bob Dylan. The riddle—the name of a fictional town in the film—is never solved. "Blowin' in the Wind," the song that first made Dylan a star, asked a series of questions for which there are no answers. How many roads? How many seas? Years? Ears? Deaths? It's all blowin' in the wind. And so go his personae. As Dylan was allowing his image to be fragmented for the silver screen in select art houses, he was also consolidating, refining, even merging them. Out of many, . . . many. After getting advised by his oldest son, Jesse, an independent filmmaker, and his blood-brother manager Jeff Rosen, Dylan signed off on the project, giving full access to his many songs and lives. He never once interfered or even inquired about the film—giving Haynes, as the filmmaker pointed out, the kind of rare creative freedom Dylan enjoys himself.

As Dylan was letting Haynes go for broke, he was also conducting several hours of interviews with Rosen that would be given to Martin Scorsese to use in a PBS documentary (*No Direction Home*, 2005) for which Scorsese would receive a director credit. Around that time, Scorsese also went down to the Delta to make a blues documentary. This would be different, a project that wouldn't require him to leave his studio. After the deaths of Stanley Kubrick and Robert Altman, Scorsese survived as a beacon of cinephilia, one of America's last great auteurs, a filmmaker known to be nervous, violent, and impatient; he talks fast and his films move even faster. Sometimes he seems to tire of a song in the middle of a scene and switches the station until the mojo is just right. To complete a viewing of *Goodfellas* (1990) or *Casino* (1995) is to be awash in a seemingly infinite playlist. You imagine Scorsese speeding down the FDR Drive, about to get into a wreck, before taking you where you didn't even realize you needed to go. He was at his most original—and most imitated—when he had a soundtrack and knew just how to manipulate it. This was evident as early as *Mean Streets* (1973), when he panned a dimly lit bar full of chiaroscuro lowlifes to the strains of The Rolling Stones' "Jumpin' Jack Flash." Scorsese was filming *The Last Waltz* (1978), The Band's star-studded farewell to the stage, in 1976, the year of *Taxi Driver.* The Band started out as Ronnie Hawkins's backup group but got famous as Dylan's, so it was appropriate that they started the night with Hawkins and finished with Dylan. Scorsese would later recall that Dylan, thinking he was talking *auteur* to *auteur,* suggested that the director check out Rainer Werner Fassbinder's *Beware of a Holy Whore.* "That was a film about the collective idea, and about its impossibility," recalled Scorsese.[1] Within a couple of years, Dylan not only had a failed marriage but a failed movie in the mostly unloved *Renaldo and Clara* (1978), which, in the spirit of Fassbinder, tried to achieve a collective correlative but, unlike Fassbinder, failed to achieve it. But Dylan was lauded as the *pièce de résistance* in *The Last Waltz*. He burned on the screen, brightly enough to provide a climax for Scorsese in 1978; and he gave his name to the Dylan documentary in 2005, one that scrutinized five years—elegantly, beautifully, compellingly—in over two hours. By the time Haynes was given the keys to the kingdom, Scorsese's film was one of many reference points. Everything was a parody, but everything was also dead serious. When Haynes poked at the myth, it was only after he had absorbed it thoroughly.

I'm Not There is a fascinating example of one artist allowed to tap into the unconscious of another. Access often spells limits, but for Haynes, access allowed him to take as weird a trip as he wanted. But his film wasn't just a triumph of its medium; it gives us a way to examine how Dylan allowed himself to be seen, and also a jumping-off point to look back on nearly half a century of head-scratchers. If Dylan had been more consistent in his image and less elusive in his music, we might not be talking about him all these years later. It is certain that a path is being laid for that sad day after Dylan gives his final encore. We don't even want to think about it, but Dylan, who keeps his decades of repertoire fresh by constantly changing keys (to accommodate his increasingly narrow range), instruments (from guitar to piano and then occasionally back to guitar), and religions, is aware that as he keeps on wheezing out the hits around 100 times a year, his exit strategy has never been clearer. Dylan studies in the university will continue, and his music will be blared in cars, in bedrooms, on commercials, in movies, and in perpetual fantasies. The Dylan hero is often the figure who said what every wronged person wanted to say, but couldn't, an idiot wind that blows forever. Scorsese's 2005 documentary is a dish served cold, a pox on those who scolded Dylan for daring to change. For an artist who began his career protesting, his most fervent protests have been against his earlier selves and the audience who wanted to embalm him in them. "He who is not being born is busy dying," goes the famous Dylan phrase. Haynes's film demonstrated the ecstasy of multiplicity. It took many decades and many reels of footage to get there.

This Film Should Be Played Loud!

Haynes had six Dylans to work with. For *The Last Waltz* (1978), Scorsese could work with only one, and he had no idea which one to expect. Dylan sounded so intimate and subtle on *Blood on the Tracks* (1975) and *Desire* (1976), the last two albums he had released. Scorsese probably wished he had filmed them, although the songs were cinematic on their own. (Whatever you think about the case of Hurricane Carter, the opening lines of "Hurricane" shoot out like a compelling action flick.) "I kissed goodbye the howling beast on the borderline which separated you from me," sang Dylan on "Idiot Wind." Perhaps, but the howling beast on stage was just getting started. Scorsese would later recall that he was, standing by stage right, terrified by Dylan's sheer volume and needed to be encouraged just to stay there. The first time Scorsese confronted Dylan, he was scared shitless. This intimidation, keep in mind, was after Scorsese had already creepily played a homicidal passenger in *Taxi Driver* who asks Robert DeNiro what a .44 Magnum could "do to a woman's pussy." Bobby DeNiro and Harvey Keitel were pals and colleagues, but *Dylan?* Scorsese could do a convincing cameo as a killer, but he was really a nervous Italian-American boy with a bad case of asthma.

Nevertheless, even when he adapted Edith Wharton's *Age of In-*

nocence (1993) or filmed *Kundun* (1997), an elaborate biopic of the Dalai Lama, Scorsese was still making movies about gangsters. There are endless grabs for power, as deadly as a Verdi opera and as beautifully orchestrated. Scorsese gives us killers we root for, sometimes in spite of ourselves. Nearly every shot is predetermined, and even when an actor improvises—most famously in Robert DeNiro's "You talkin' to me?" riff in *Taxi Driver*—little is left to chance. For *The Last Waltz*, Scorsese wrote storyboards for every song. Rick Danko is nearly blinded by a spotlight when he sings about getting lost in one. Such moments are so impeccably crafted that they are not crass literalism but objective correlative.

Still, this was The Band's project, not his. The fast-talking perfectionist from NYU film school was directing not his own actors but musical subjects with plans of their own. None drove a harder bargain than Dylan. He came on as the finale after over seven hours of music—from The Band, Van Morrison, Neil Young, Joni Mitchell, and many more—and he only nailed down an agreement with the nervous director shortly before he blazed through after 2 a.m. This was a long way from the split-screen chaos of *Woodstock* (1970), for which Scorsese was a co-editor when he was just starting out. And yet chaos would come again.

Around the time *The Last Waltz* was released, Dylan came out with his own *Renaldo and Clara*, a nearly four-hour film that remained only slightly longer in movie theatres. (The film still has no official video or DVD release.) *Renaldo and Clara* had its moments. All of the musical scenes featuring Dylan were stunning. And a staged conversation between Dylan and Allen Ginsberg at Jack Kerouac's grave is well worth the trek to Lowell. Dylan conducts lively street interviews about Hurricane Carter in Harlem. But the improv with amateur actors—including Sara, Dylan's soon to be ex-wife—is often incoherent, and it turned out that spontaneity was harder than it looked. Joan Baez, a constant presence in the film as siren, muse, and wisecracker, was merciless when she assessed the work in progress. "The movie needs a director," Baez declared. "The sense I get out of it so far is that that movie is a giant mess of a home movie" (Heylin 2001, 138). Where were Robert Altman or John Cassavetes when you needed them? Sam Shepard, who was on board as "co-screenwriter" without an actual script, was a truly great playwright who was perhaps too involved behind the scenes, and too much in awe of Dylan to tell the king that he could not lead his own tour, imbibe in the libations of the moment, and also direct a great experimental film. Something had to give. Scorsese's storyboarding looked increasingly wise in retrospect.

Dylan, uneasy about possible competition between *Renaldo and Clara* and *The Last Waltz* (he might as well have worried about *Heaven's Gate*), first refused to allow any songs to be filmed. Scorsese was suddenly not directing a gangster picture but living in one. Dylan balked at appearing on screen. After prodding and guilt-tripping from Robbie Robertson, he finally relented. Out of a four-song set, he allowed only two: "Forever Young" and a reprise of the folk standard "Baby, Let Me Follow You Down," which had been featured on both Dylan's first album and every night of The Band's 1976 tour. When Scorsese asked Dylan's road manager, Ron Stone, if he would get a signal for when to start shooting, he was told, "Well yeah, kind of." One would never know it from how artfully Scorsese pans down from that oversized fedora to Dylan at thirty-five, sporting one of the fullest beards he would ever wear in public. His outfit was like a 1976 variation of 1965, polka-dot shirt, leather jacket, jeans, just a little wider on the neck and the flare. Every movement, every gesture seems to say, okay, you can have me. Because I am letting you.

After his delicate, almost ponderous guitar introduction to what turns out to be "Forever Young," The Band—even though they were playing a ballad—explode with fury. Scorsese, who created operas of violence on the splattering silver screen, could not take such an assault on his poor ears. "When he came on, it was so loud on the stage that I didn't know what to do," Scorsese recalled later. "Bill Graham was next to me saying, 'Shoot him! He comes from the same streets as you. Don't worry, don't let him push you around, shoot him'" (Christie and Thompson 2003, 75). Dylan came from the Iron Range, not Little Italy, but in Scorsese's world, a gangster is a gangster. It took the tough-as-nails concert promoter Bill Graham, owner of San Francisco's Winterland, where the concert was mounted, to give him the kind of talk heard from boxing trainers— in the movies. For Scorsese to get his final storyboards in the flesh, he had to become Raging Bull.

Dylan's off-camera rendition of "Hazel" sounded pleasingly rough but not ready for prime time. This time, the camera made him better, perhaps because he knew he was being shot by a serious filmmaker. The Rolling Stones had Godard, the Beatles had Richard Lester, even the Dave Clark Five had John Boorman. Dylan had had D. A. Pennebaker to capture lightning in a bottle for two documentaries, but Scorsese was different. With his units of cameras operated by the best in the business, an artfully lit opera set, and hot Italian blood, Scorsese could make it rain. Once Scorsese could absorb all his noise, it was clear that Dylan was on. He'd been rehearsing this part for a long time, and he provided quite the spontaneous story arc. After the first verse, he turns to someone who appears to be Scorsese himself. (Robbie Robertson and Rick Danko are on the other side, and Levon Helm on drums is too far behind.) He looks into the camera and gives the most blasé shrug imaginable, as if to say, This stuff I got'll bust your brains out, baby, but I really don't care. Then, after the second verse, he sees someone in the audience. The person isn't visible, but it is obviously someone Dylan likes very much. He points, gives a full-toothed smile (a true rarity) and smiles through the chorus, barely able to contain himself. Robbie plays a solo that is best described as electric flamenco. It looks hard, but what the hell? A little later, Dylan turns to Robbie. You can read his lips saying "Seventh chord." Robbie looks determined and exhausted, sweat dripping through his half-opened shirt, evidence that he has, after all, been playing for seven hours. Dylan's only been up there for half an hour.

D major becomes D seventh. Levon Helm is looking up, wondering what is coming next. Rick Danko gives a Cheshire Cat grin when he figures it out, looking a little like a lanky long-haired DeNiro from *Mean Streets*. The song is "Baby, Let Me Follow You Down," but Dylan is defiantly leading. At one point, he turns sharply with an almost balletic precision, but the camera is still there. In 1966, Dylan and the Hawks were booed at every venue where they played the song. In 1962, Dylan was still "Hammond's Folly" when he first recorded it for his inauspicious debut. Now they were treated like heroes. After an anthemic "I Shall Be Released" where the two Neils (Diamond and Young) staked out separate mic space by the second verse, joined by Joni Mitchell, Van Morrison, and even Ringo on drums (but where was Muddy Waters?), Dylan walks off stage, not to be seen again until the "alimony tour" of *Street-Legal*. This is the last time anyone will see him like this. And it is the last time anyone will ever see The Band with its original lineup. Except, of course, at the movies. And this one, lest anyone forget Dylan's challenge to Scorsese, begins with an unmistakable directive: "This film should be played loud!"

The Last Temptation of Dylan

If in *The Last Waltz* Scorsese had to impose order onto chaos by storyboarding a concert that repeatedly threatened to go out of control, something of the reverse happened when he was approached to direct a Dylan documentary twenty-five years later.

Over time, the film became a classic: all those cameras, all that neurosis, all the madness could now be seen as a manic victory lap. Since their work together, Scorsese had employed Robbie Robertson as a music supervisor on several films, from *Raging Bull* (1980) to *Shutter Island* (2010). For Scorsese and Dylan, *The Last Waltz* was only the beginning. Dylan's music resurfaced in Scorsese's work most dramatically in "Life Lessons" (1989), a short film about an artist (Nick Nolte), his young assistant (Rosanna Arquette), and their stormy affair. She provides youth and beauty, he provides proximity to greatness. Needless to say, the affair ends badly. The film's most memorable moment is its climactic scene of painting through the stormy breakup. Dylan and The Band's 1974 *Before the Flood* performance of "Like a Rolling Stone" seems to guide the frenetic camera work as Arquette, as she is about to walk out the door, is still mesmerized by her old lover's brushstrokes, transfixed by his frenzied swirls, splotches, and flourishes. "How does it feel?" asks a familiar refrain, made less familiar by the rough, sloppy, and sublime performance. Without the music, it would be cliché— a May-December romance, Pygmalion, artist and pupil, old man and coquettish young blonde, art over life. Yet the sound of Dylan makes it impossible to look away. Scorsese makes the jagged motions, the vertiginous sweeps that demonstrate how a Dylan recording can find new vitality if the suspense is staged just right. Such scenes—especially when they were just music—were played loud, and gloriously.

No Direction Home (2005) is in many ways a departure from the Scorsese method, yet it still contains his inimitable narrative flourishes. Even though he did not actually film a single frame, it still feels, as advertised, like a "Martin Scorsese Picture." What, under such conditions, is the distinction between directing and merely signing? While it is true that Scorsese conducted none of the interviews and shot none of the footage, this is largely the case with

Orson Welles's *F for Fake* (1975), which is based mostly on the footage of François Reichenbach and is considered to be Welles's last major completed film. Norman Mailer's Pulitzer Prize–winning book *The Executioner's Song* (1980) leaned heavily on interviews conducted by Lawrence Schiller. As the years go by, the collaborations and appropriations become reduced to a historical footnote, and the works, if they hold up, fatten the oeuvre. As he did in *The Last Waltz*, Scorsese takes what is normally in the background and makes it explode with fury and demand attention until it becomes foreground—yet it only enhances the narrative. He has a knack for pumping up the volume in a way that feeds the action. When, for example, a coked-up Ray Liotta in *Goodfellas* (1990) is speeding through New Jersey accompanied by fragments of Muddy Waters and the Rolling Stones, the music and plot are one. *No Direction Home* was both easier—no one to interview, nothing to stage—and harder: how do you take footage from elsewhere and make it yours?

Scorsese's strategy was, in a sense, to make yet another mobster film. The adversaries are in a battle between stasis and change, tradition and inspiration. Along with the folkie furies, there are the clueless reporters expecting straight answers from an artist who dwells in opacities. The star of this movie resembles Willem Dafoe's title character in Scorsese's *Last Temptation of Christ* (1988). He's an unorthodox Jew with a lot of controversial things to say, first in the language of the ancients (in Dylan's case, Woody, Hank, Muddy, Leadbelly, Odetta, and so on), then in his own. When, in Manchester in May 1966, he is condemned from the balcony as "Judas," the best retort, after his famous reaction ("I don't believe you. You're a liar."), played "fucking loud" as he instructed his band, is "Like a Rolling Stone." How does it feel to be staging a pogrom? And was he, as Ron Rosenbaum wondered, Judas to his own Jesus? Scorsese's Dylan endures torture and incomprehension just to rock his message. First he's famous, then he's infamous. They loved him, they hated him, they went after him, they'd learn to love him again and repeat. Young keyboard player Al Kooper begs off the tour because when he sees Dallas on the itinerary, he wonders if Dylan will be the next JFK and get shot. Yet this is a martyr who lives—a Jesus who will eventually find Christ, but not in this movie. This was to be a standoff between Dylan and his public; he was moving too fast. If they were watching the documentary, they had probably caught up. Just a year later, Jimi Hendrix covered "Like a Rolling Stone" at Monterey and not only played scorching electric guitar, but played it with his teeth, then set it on fire. Everyone howled for more. There is no summary judgment of what followed in rock music just a year later, which would have dated—and deflated—the intensity.

The Dylan of this film always gets the last, withering word. ("Here he is," he says of himself backstage, strapping on his electric guitar. "Back from the grave.") This could be propaganda for Dylan, but it is also immensely satisfying and at least selectively true. The framing device was the voluminous footage shot by D. A. Pennebaker— who was filming *Eat the Document*, his never-released follow-up to *Dont Look Back*—following Dylan's 1966 European tour with the Hawks, the proto-Band, with drummer Levon Helm replaced by Mickey Jones. After a single anecdote from childhood, most of the narrative is from 1961, the beginning of Dylan's career, to 1966, when he went electric and got met with a chorus of boos everywhere he went. We watch this footage persuaded that Dylan was not only a genius but a misunderstood one, and it is precisely this tension that permits Scorsese to work his narrative powers. As the documentary opens, we see Dylan performing the classic rock warhorse "Like a Rolling Stone." The record had already been a number-two single, but in 1966 it was still a rock-and-roll *Rite of Spring*, too raw for the purists. You know you are in the hands of an *auteur* and not a PBS hack when, midverse, just when Dylan is about to snarl more adenoidal invective to Miss Lonely, Scorsese cuts to a frigid, silent Minnesota wilderness. The scene conveys a visceral feeling of Dylan defiantly inventing himself by escaping his past, not out of Abe and Beatty Zimmerman's middle-class Jewish home but out of a bleak nothingness filled only by a wafting, distant radio playing Bill Monroe's "Drifting Too Far from the Shore." Dylan, sounding like a crotchety grandpa, recalls that the winters were "rightly cold" and that he "didn't have the clothes you have now. It was so cold, you couldn't be bad." Young Bobby Zimmerman was bad enough, though, stealing folk records from a collector friend in the name of being a "musical expeditionary." Steve Allen asks Dylan if he sings his own material or other people's. He replies: "They're all mine, now."

Scorsese's Dylan begins as a rebel without a cause—until he finds one pretty quickly. Before he finds Jack Kerouac and then, crucially, Woody Guthrie, his adolescent inertia is played for irony. On his semester at the University of Minnesota: "I didn't go to classes . . . I just didn't feel like it." On changing his name: "I mean, I just don't feel like I had a past and I couldn't relate to anything other than what I was doing at the present time and it didn't matter to me what I said. It still doesn't, really." But there's no doubt that it mattered to him a great deal when he found his "singing partner" Joan Baez or belted out that "the whole wide world is watchin'" at the same podium where King would deliver his "I Had a Dream" speech—an event that "affects me to this day." Dylan cared, but he cared just long enough for it to matter. So we see, just as he had written "Song to Woody," that he had to move away from Woody; that soon after Joan Baez helped him with his career, he would surely not help her with hers (his justification—"You can't be wise and in love at the same time"—makes sense only from the author of "Don't Think Twice It's Alright"). He couldn't hang around all those earnest folkniks when other, louder, nastier forms of inspiration called. Just when you're seduced by the righteousness of Dylan organizing black voters in Mississippi with Pete Seeger and singing a wise jeremiad about the assassination of Medgar Evers, you are jerked back to 1966, the film's primary cultural space, where he is called, in various forms of youthful cockney, "Traitor!" a "fake neurotic," "rank," "lousy," "pathetic" and is accused of "prostituting himself." One pimply young man summed up the electric portion of Dylan's concerts: "Bob Dylan was a bastard in the second half." And what a cinematic bastard he was. This is the 1966 version of political correctness. We watch fragments of each song from the electric set and let history be the judge.

Joan Baez explains that she had believed that sex, drugs, and rock and roll were "wicked." A bummer like that can't have the last word. Or can she? Scorsese's film seduces us into believing in Dylan as a rock-and-roll martyr, someone who seemed destined to become a rock-and-roll suicide. Sex is barely hinted at in this documentary, and drugs are present only in his unmistakably altered presentation at press conferences that seem pretty miserable to endure sober. The film allows us to feel Baez's pain while still following—indeed honoring—Dylan's trajectory. Baez was too prim for Dylan's rock-and-roll lifestyle of 1965, but in this film she is singing a version of "Love Is Just a Four-Letter Word" with her vocal chops intact. She stole that song from Dylan back then, and forty years later, with this haunting performance she nearly steals *No Direction Home* too, not a bad revenge for being publicly jilted in *Dont Look Back*. Over the years, she has gained thicker skin and an acerbic wit. Throughout the interviews, she curses like a sailor and jabs Dylan with deft comic timing. Only after it was over did she learn to laugh at it all and gain a different kind of self-possession. When they were on the Rolling Thunder Revue together in 1975–76, she would describe him to audiences as "by far, the most talented crazy person I ever worked with." Even in Scorsese's film, her memory of him still burns. She still obviously has it bad for the guy, and this movie seduces us into understanding why. "I don't know what he thought about," Baez says. "I only know what he gave us."

Bricolage on Bricolage

Todd Haynes also had an idea of what Dylan gave us, but it was radically different from anyone else's. At the end of *I'm Not There* (2007), his multiple-personality biopic of Dylan, we are given a shock of the old. We follow hordes among a 1966 English crowd ready to crucify him in the electric set, an activity that was the framing device for *No Direction Home*. At the end of Haynes's film we get something more reverential, less controversial: the simple image and sound of Dylan playing harmonica on an acoustic "Mr. Tambourine Man." We gasp at the simple image of breathing, because Dylan has been everywhere and nowhere in Haynes's project. His music is ubiquitous, but his image and name cannot be found. The film disjointedly patches together six narratives about people who only have a connection under the concept "Bob Dylan." The deeper we go into artifice, the more shocking it is to confront the man himself. It is the transfiguration of the commonplace. Myriad versions of "Mr. Tambourine Man" from decade after decade are readily available on YouTube, hulu, and bobdylan.com, not to mention iTunes and even record, cassette, and CD collections from back in the day. Dylan is easily found, yet hard to fathom. Haynes's film provides an incandescence that is at once familiar and uncanny. The more mysterious he is, the more it causes a flutter to actually see Bob Dylan himself, in a musical circle. He doesn't speak or sing, he just breathes into his harmonica, a jagged major chord variation with no beginning or end. For two hours, Haynes hijacks our imaginations with the ballad of the six Dylans. By the time it winds down, the Dylan who appears at the end is nothing less than the return of the repressed.

How did Haynes do it? How was he able, in the opening credits, to show archival footage of the New York subway in the 1960s while making "Stuck Inside of Mobile with the Memphis Blues Again" sound raw, rough, and even a little dangerous? Haynes takes Scorsese's propaganda and raises it, tapping into the Dylanesque unconscious—equal parts biography, myth, dream, and musical saturation. In some ways he has been here before. This is not only his third biopic but his third brazenly unconventional one, queer in every sense. Haynes came on the scene as the most audacious director of the New Queer Cinema, but like Dylan and the folkies, he could not be reduced to an ideology. It is no accident that Haynes was a semiotics major at Brown. Floating signifiers are everywhere in his debut film, *Superstar: The Karen Carpenter Story* (1987), in which Karen and her brother Richard Carpenter are played by Barbie and Ken dolls that somehow, on a graduate student's budget (the film was an MFA thesis at Bard), elicit tears from his viewers. What started as playing with dolls becomes pity and terror. The anorexic doll and its soft rock soundtrack evoked childhood for viewers of a certain age—the right age, it turned out—as much as it provided a sublime artifice with real emotions.

After the bootleg-only phenomenon of *Superstar*, Haynes went legit, sort of. *Poison* (1991) was a potent AIDS allegory, and its format of three overlapping, seemingly disconnected narratives foreshadowed what he would double with *I'm Not There*. *Safe* (1995) was another illness-as-metaphor that, with Julianne Moore's stunning performance, went deeply into the psyche of a shallow but troubled and delicate soul, another withering Barbie. Many assumed that the illness was AIDS, but Haynes brought on the indeterminacy when he said, "*Safe* is on the side of the disease and not the cure," deepening the soul of a blithe, vulnerable woman. *Velvet Goldmine* (1998), Haynes's second weird musical biopic, took something of a step back artistically, but not for lack of ambition. The film was both a glam rock mystery and a *Citizen Kane* homage, but the entire project hinged on the brief period when David Bowie was proudly bisexual. (Bowie was an icon of androgyny about as long as Dylan was a protest singer—long enough to reap the benefits and move on.) Haynes was not even trying to make a biopic about David Bowie but about Ziggy Stardust. Bowie wanted no part of revisiting the era of "God-given ass" for any price, and without his music, it felt hollow, bereft. Despite its many splendors, this was not a simulacrum that worked, and Haynes would never let that happen to him again. After channeling Douglas Sirk right down to the Elmer Bernstein score and every other weepy 1950s detail in *Far from Heaven* (2002), he found his way into an obsession with Dylan that matched his obsessions with Sirk, Bowie, and Karen Carpenter.

Consistent with his New Queer Cinema origins, he took the one period in 1965–66 captured in D. A. Pennebaker's *Dont Look Back* and *Eat the Document* in which Dylan was genuinely androgynous, probably unassumingly so. Haynes never suggests that Dylan had gay experiences, just that he had a female self, one that was uncannily played by the indefatigable Cate Blanchett, whose performance scored an Oscar nomination and a Golden Globe. Haynes said he was fascinated with the "feline quality" of this period of Dylan, and you find yourself simultaneously believing in Blanchett's interpretation and appreciating its audacity. Dylan also—and this is more obvious—had a black self, a symbolist poet self, an outlaw self, a misogynistic matinee idol self, and, for a spell, a preacher self. *I'm Not There* gets them all. The film begins with a death, a tongue-in-cheek elegy delivering lines from Dylan's associative and dashed-off novel *Tarantula* (1971) from the gravelly voice of Kris Kristofferson. "Only the dead can be born again," says Kristofferson, and what emerges is indeed a rebirth as we see the fragmented selves of Dylan anew. Despite this morbid introduction, this is not a film about death. A rock-and-roll suicide is a tighter narrative, one that we have seen too often. Life in all its messy splendor, especially the life of a mind and a soul capable of embodying genuine weirdness from so many personae, is a more elusive phenomenon that is somehow captured by Haynes and his ever-changing lenses (Super 8 for the 1960s, of course). The death at the beginning shows us what could easily have happened in 1966. Whether or not that motorcycle crash was all it was cracked up to be, there is no question that Dylan was moving way too fast, ingesting too many drugs, and riding so high—even amid the boos—that there seemed to be only one way to go. Besides, he could barely drive that bike.

Yet what follows is a never-ending tour of sorts, a boxcar waiting to be hopped on. Haynes's bag of tricks is an amalgam of the Dylan songs he loves, covers by his favorite indie artists, and images from his favorite 1960s films. The film is so jam-packed with homages to Jean-Luc Godard, Federico Fellini, and Richard Lester (especially an intertextual love affair with *Petulia*) and saturated with dialogue taken from Dylan lyrics and interviews, as well as lines from Rimbaud (the name of Ben Wishaw's chain-smoking fey poet) and others, Haynes even confessed, "I don't think there's anything from the script that's actually my own." Like Dylan, who especially in his later work clipped everything from Ovid to Bing Crosby, and like Godard, who in *Nouvelle Vague* and *Histoire(s) du Cinema* realized Walter Benjamin's model of quotation as discourse, Haynes realized that rather than inventing dialogue for a realist Dylan, he could be freed by pastiche and come closer to his subject. Dylan obsessives will find something for them, whether it is a literalized image of a lyric (there is a young child beside a dead pony) or quotations from various Dylan interviews and biographies. But the non-obsessives can also find a way to become a little more obsessed, because Haynes is showing you the thrill of discovery, a Dylan who needn't be reduced to a single self, and a vision that doesn't have to conform to time or space but to the best that has been thought and shot by the

1960s film mavericks, whose images were as startling in their way as Dylan's music. The idea is liberation, impersonation as freedom.

But the lack of fixed identity comes at a price. The figure in the Dylan songs that reverberate most powerfully (as opposed to the charming but less compelling songs celebrating domestic bliss) is the rambler, the gambler, the outlaw. As in music, and as in life, so too in *I'm Not There:* things fall apart. The title track, an outtake from *The Basement Tapes* given its first official release on the film's soundtrack, is in part about dramatizing absence. The self of the song is a fantasy. Some of the lyrics are unfinished—clearly, certain words are placeholders. But these words are unmistakable: "I wish I was beside her but I'm not there, I'm gone"; then at the end: "I wish I was there to help her but I'm not there I'm gone." The way he sings it, as emotionally raw as he would ever be, it's hard to know whether to be moved by his wish to be beside the woman in the song, or whether it is his absence that is truly sad. Dylan, blissfully deluded that he is singing in private, is singing an open wound, but who is the wounded? He is, after all, not there. Or is he everywhere? We can't weep for the Dylan figure any more than we can for his jilted lovers or betrayed friends. He keeps moving on to the next thing, which can't be easy for those who want to move with him but can't. We didn't need Todd Haynes to tell us that, but we do need him to take it to the movies.

This is why Heath Ledger's performance as Robbie Clark hits where it hurts, yet the effect is somehow gorgeous. Ledger lost a lot of sleep preparing for this role, which only heightened the pharmaceutical intake that would kill him at twenty-eight, months after the film's release. It is impossible to watch this performance without a sense of foreboding. Beauty walks a razor's edge. Most of the time, Clark is an inconsiderate bastard, a misogynist cursed with beauty and talent. In his early scenes, he's the young lover patterned after the cover of *Freewheelin'* with Dylan strolling the Village with Suze

Rotolo. In the end, Ledger fleshes out the ghostly image of Paul Till's cover portrait for *Blood on the Tracks*. When Haynes channeled Douglas Sirk, he mined melodrama. These Robbie Clark scenes are largely allusive of Godard, especially *Two or Three Things I Know About Her* . . . . Haynes has a Godardian look with a melodramatic soul, which is not a bad metaphor for the disorienting songwriting techniques on *Blood on the Tracks*. Dylan, who was a painting student of Norman Raeben's at the time, was fascinated by how, in painting, one can create multiple time periods on the same canvas. It is useful to know this when decoding "Tangled Up in Blue" and "Idiot Wind," and Haynes's jumps in the space-time continuum give us a way of seeing how deep, tragic emotions can be spliced and diced. How many times can you be walked out upon? Or do the walking? The emotion is so painful, it needs to be cut up and moved back and forth. One minute you're at the topless bar and the next you recall living with a slave dealer on Montague Street. The song goes hither and thither, but ends on a grand climax, painting and entangling everyone in blue. Haynes works in a similar way. As much as he bewilders you, he brings it back home.

Of course, just because Dylan travels through time, he is not immune to its ravages. He ages like anyone else, but he also mutates and even exfoliates. Creeds and schools in abeyance. Race, gender, orientation, electric, acoustic, atheist, leftist, female, misogynist, hobo, Jewish, Christian—all these categories are exploded here, and in the spirit in which Dylan explodes them. Whitman, New Queer Poet of the American Renaissance, contained multitudes. In *I'm Not There*, Dylan's multitudes contain multitudes. In real life, those multitudes accumulated over time. Every three years he turned into someone else, and every time he changed, his audience was nostalgic for three years earlier. This happened consistently between 1963 and 1966 (folkie to surrealist rocker), 1966–69 (rocker to countrified Cash acolyte), 1976–79 (messianic rocker to converso Christian), 1979–83 (Evangelical Christian to Zionist Jew), and so on. There may be those who think that *Together Through Life* (2009) is a decline from *Modern Times* (2006), but the rancor has cleared for now, despite some surprise about *Christmas in the Heart* (2009). What makes Haynes's film radical is that he gives us what we already have, but he shows us how uncanny it all is. When you dramatize these aspects of Dylan alongside each other, with the logic of a dream as opposed to a standard rock biography, the changes are no longer changes but simultaneous experiences that all lead to the same songs, the same eccentricity, the same lies and myths, the same beauty and confusion. This is not the inevitable Dylan of classic rock radio. This makes the case that looking at Dylan is a new way of looking at existence. You can be all races, all genders, live in various historical fantasies, be shot by the cinematographer of your dreams. There is only one thing left to say once we leave the town of Riddle for good and see the man behind the personae. It is a question we have been hearing for years yet never fully answered, one that follows a strident drumbeat and an inescapable organ line: How does it feel?

What Things Don't Mean

Scorsese and Haynes brought Dylan-approved material to the screen. Dylan made his own attempt to do the same with *Masked and Anonymous* (2003), directed by Larry Charles (of *Seinfeld* and *Curb Your Enthusiasm* fame) and co-written by Charles and Dylan (credited to Sergei Petrov and Rene Fontaine). As in *Renaldo and Clara*, the musical performances (actually performed live on screen, a treat) are phenomenal. But also as in *Renaldo and Clara*, the associative allegory that drives many a great Dylan song sputters on the screen. *New York Times* film critic A. O. Scott, who elsewhere had written that he loved Bob Dylan so much he was daunted by the prospect of coming up with the right words of praise, summed up his vexation about being a Dylan exegete and a film critic: "As a movie, 'Masked & Anonymous,' directed by Larry Charles, a master of the sitcom domain making his big-screen debut, is an unholy, incoherent mess. As a Bob Dylan artifact, though, it is endlessly, perhaps morbidly, fascinating" (Scott, *New York Times*, July 24, 2003). The movie had its defenders, including indie film god Jim Jarmusch, and to those of us who were trying to understand Dylan, if it helped us unload his head, it was a train wreck well worth watching.

Set in an apocalyptic banana republic that looks like a garbage-strewn East LA, where "Like a Rolling Stone" is reconceived as an Italian rap with scratchy Dylan samples, *Masked and Anonymous* is both alienating and familiar. Pros and genuine stoics, including Jessica Lange, Jeff Bridges, Bruce Dern, Mickey Rourke, Penelope Cruz, and John Goodman, all do their best to make their stilted dialogue sound spontaneous. Dylan plays a character called Jack Fate, who was a rock star before being sent to prison for unexplained reasons. His father is a dying Latin dictator (with a Jewish son boasting a Vincent Price mustache and cowboy hat), the kind of corrupt guy who keeps Amnesty International in business. Here's the good news: Jack has to play a televised concert (after they couldn't get Sting, Billy Joel, or Paul McCartney), which means he has to rehearse for it. The performances of "Down in the Flood," "I'll Remember You," "Drifter's Escape," "Cold Irons Bound," and even a counterintuitive "Dixie" are stunning, and they move the scenes along with their raspy power. Many of the talented actors play characters who do not live and breathe, yet they pontificate and philosophize. One, a scraggly makeshift zoo keeper played by Val Kilmer, speaks in an affected southern dialect (he is no longer playing Jim Morrison) about how animals don't try to be anything other than what they are, but man feels the need to try on identities of others. Dylan stands there just listening—in his reality, in this film, conversations consist of one hand clapping. The Dylan of Scorsese and Haynes juggles identities; not so in this movie. Speaking of the purity of God's wild kingdom, Kilmer, a St. Francis of this rancid studio lot, says, "They're just beautiful because they are. Lion don't try to be tiger. Rabbit don't try to do an impression of a monkey. They don't try to be what they're not. . . . Then man came in. Who created him and for what purpose: still a mystery. Why is he here? It's a mystery. We know he's trespassing. Doesn't know his own place. . . . Masked and anonymous. No one truly knows 'im." This rant against civilization could, if set to verse, resemble a Luddite anthem like "License to Kill" from *Infidels*. The animal keeper does not speak for Dylan; he represents the opposite of Dylan's protean survival strategy. Dylan is the "shape-shifter," according to Liam Clancy in *No Direction Home*. He is not a turtle that will stay in its shell.

And yet, this wacky monologue, which becomes increasingly incoherent before it sputters out, provides the title and perhaps the guiding metaphor of the film. (Instead of six Dylans, there's only one, reluctant, like God, to appear.) Every time the real Dylan has donned a mask, he was never exactly anonymous. "I'm not there, I'm gone," is absence as presence. Yet this is a journey into the Dylanesque unconscious, courtesy of Dylan himself. Perhaps dispersing his thoughts around these broad characters might have diluted the magic. "It's Halloween," Dylan said at a 1964 concert, "I've got my Bob Dylan mask on." He would later title an undistinguished album *Empire Burlesque* (1985). What worked in songs, even their cinematic quality, did not survive cinema itself. And yet the panning of the film by most critics did not dent Dylan's standing as a major cultural entity, and its most privileged moments demonstrate why. Even in this Desolation Row, Dylan makes some perceptive comments about his real career as a veteran rock star. At one point, the promoter Nina Veronica (Jessica Lange), worried about

Fate's abilities after all these years, tells Uncle Sweetheart (John Goodman), "You can't compare the here and now to the there and then. I don't care what he's done in the past." When she asks if his songs will be recognizable, Sweetheart replies, "All of his songs are recognizable even when they're not recognizable." Anyone who has gone to a Dylan concert since he plugged in would recognize this conversation. Dylan recognizes it, too, and gives it back, and in a movie that's not so easy to parse, either.

A moment when Dylan's performance holds a completely baffling moment together is when he leads his band in an impassioned rendition of "Dixie," Daniel Decatur Emmet's mid-nineteenth-century paean to the Confederacy, perhaps the most popular song in the history of blackface minstrelsy. Dylan is unearthing America's sins to a carnival audience. Freak-show versions of Gandhi, Pope John Paul, Abe Lincoln, and others congregate in a world where everything is inverted. (Dylan's favorite childhood place in boring old Hibbing was the circus, where he recalled seeing George Washington and Abe Lincoln in blackface.) Various African Americans, including a guy in a Rastafarian cap, seem moved. Something's happening here and we're not sure what it is, but it includes a well-turned irony. Dylan uncovers everything in America, even the ugliest history set to the catchiest tune. There's no south and north anymore, just this weird, corrupt government where all that is left of America is kitschy debris. And yet Dylan is so impassioned as he strains to hit the high notes. He puts every fiber of his being into it, as if he was singing "Visions of Johanna" for the first time. There is nothing overtly racist in the lyrics Dylan sings. One cannot, after all, escape one's origins. (In Dylan's case: middle class, Jewish, Midwestern, but never mind.) Perhaps he is trying to liberate the song from its context, with Honest Abe and Gandhi envisioning a new Dixie of the mind. (And didn't The Band essentially do this thematically with "The Night They Drove Old Dixie Down"? And didn't leftist goddess Joan Baez do the same with her top-ten cover version?) Joyce's Stephen Dedalus said history was a nightmare from which he was trying to awake. Dylan's "Dixie" does not celebrate nightmares but stands in ironic defiance against them. There are several African Americans in the audience, but no one calls him Judas. They all applaud on cue.

"You ever heard of cellulose? Cows can digest it, but you can't. And neither can I." Jack Fate utters this biological fact apropos of nothing. Whitman was untranslatable. Dylan, according to his character, is perhaps undigestible, at least in this movie. Jeff Bridges is appropriately weaselly as Tom Friend, representing the worst species in this universe: the rock critic. He has convoluted riffs on various figures of the 1960s—Janis, Jimi, Zappa, Hefner—and expects Jack to answer them all. He expects him to *be* the 1960s. "I own the 60s," Dylan told *Rolling Stone* a few years after this movie. "You can have 'em." Naturally, this line of questioning makes Jack furious. First he bolts to weep (this is definitely a Visine cry) at his father's deathbed, get comfort in the obvious way from Alfrie Woodard, and then return to play a riveting version of "Cold Irons Bound," fiddling, or jamming, while Rome burns. Eventually things get worse with the rock critic, since of course all critics carry guns. He gets his just rewards, bludgeoned to death by Bobby Cupid (Luke Wilson) with a guitar that allegedly belonged to Blind Lemon Jefferson. Fate takes the rap, of course, born outlaw that he is, and he's sent right back on the same bus that brought him in. He has some new thoughts, though, and a lovely, slow guitar progression carries us along. It is from a live performance, and Dylan speaks over his own soundtrack: "Sometimes it's not enough to know the meaning of things. Sometimes we have to know what things don't mean as well. Like, what does it mean to not know what the person you love is capable of? Things fall apart, especially the neat order of rules and laws. The way we look at the world is the way we really are. Truth and beauty are in the eye of the beholder. I stopped trying to figure everything out a long time ago."

Dylan imagines a mode of inquiry that privileges "what things don't mean," a dreamlike inversion in which truth and fantasy switch places. Dylan is not the first, and will not be the last, to be against interpretation. As soon as the monologue stops, in which he managed to doff his cowboy hat to both Yeats and Keats, a sublime version of "Blowin' in the Wind" can be heard. Even though it is a version from later in life, he still sounds as if he is coming up with the lyrics for the first time, as if these decades of love and madness and disappointment and adulation have just deepened the song's philosophy. The song that first rocketed Dylan to stardom now accompanies him on the bus ride to hell. But Dylan chartered that bus, and this is only a movie. When we wake up we wonder, is that what he's been thinking all these years? Is that really how he sees himself? However baffling much of the film is, it is poignant to leave him still wondering how many roads a man must walk down. It is a question that will never have a definitive answer.

Take Two

And so we return to 1965, to that vulnerable face of new fame and youthful exhaustion. It is a face that seems to have had enough of the grind, the gig, the road—a face that wants a home. Even though he retreated to a home for eight years, a prisoner of fame whether in Woodstock or on MacDougal Street, he went back to the road and never stopped. He accumulated various properties, but home was the tour bus. He somehow gave himself a performance persona that was his and his alone, something he could hide behind, masked and anonymous in front of an arena, in the state fairs, at casinos. Pennebaker gave us the newsreel, Scorsese the ravishing spectacle,

Haynes the audacious postmodern allegory, and Dylan the shaggy-dog self-portrait. But the Warhol Screen Test was the most vulnerable, bare-boned portrait of them all, a love that spoke like silence. Dylan continues to hold his head up high, face the spotlight, play his set, introduce the band, and get the hell out. "No man sees my face and lives," Dylan once sang. He was talking about God and Moses. But he was also talking about how compelled we are to look, and how compelled he is, too. With Sam Shepard he wrote "Brownsville Girl" (1986), a spectacular homage to a Western called *The Gun-fighter*, only it wasn't just about watching the movie but wondering where he could find himself on the flickering screen. "Something about that movie though, well I just can't get it out of my head / But I can't remember why I was in it or what part I was supposed to play." Dylan conflates the Gregory Peck image with his own. It is the image on screen that makes him think about the role he is "supposed to play." Eventually, he got some ideas.

In the new millennium, Dylan finally made some calls, green-lighted some projects, made a go of it with his own. The Dylans were multiple, unruly, mythic, apocryphal. The spectator gets sucked in. She wants to know more, as if there is a "true" Dylan out there. At a twenty-first century Dylan concert, at nearly every performance, there is at least one amateur cinematographer in the audience, holding a cell phone and shakily documenting what Dylan was doing on a particular night. Warhol showed us how everybody could be a star. Now, everyone can be a filmmaker, sort of. Clearly, everybody will not be Scorsese or Haynes for fifteen minutes. But everybody will have more access to Dylan's image and performance than the brat perched before Warhol in 1965 could have imagined. That screen test, the first of many, foreshadowed projects more daunting and revealing. Yet even when he's being inundated with cell phones, high-tech autograph seekers who post their loot for all to see, there is something no one can get to, and that is just a small part of what keeps us watching. Look at that face. What is he offering? What do you want? Are you the one who truly understands the meaning of his songs? Good luck. He's not selling any alibis as you stare into the vacuum of his eyes.

THREE

Not Dark Yet

How Bob Dylan Got His Groove Back

June 7, 2004, was not just another gig for Bob Dylan. Sandwiched between one-nighters in Atlantic City and Delaware, Dylan went uptown to play the Apollo Theater, the legendary venue where Ella Fitzgerald passed the audition for the Chick Webb orchestra and where, on a 1962 live album, James Brown made a gig in Harlem a chart-topping soundtrack for the world. In black America, "Showtime at the Apollo" could make or break a career. It has traditionally been the venue where African American discourse is taken to the people, and the response is either up or down. If you're a comedian and you don't get laughs, or if you're a singer and you do, it may be the moment to go back to your day job. "Went to the Apollo, should've seen them go-go-go," sang Lou Reed on "Walk on the Wild Side," his only hit single. In the 1965 liner notes for *Bringing It All Back Home*, Dylan wrote, "the fact that the white house is filled with leaders who have never been t'the apollo theater amazes me."

The world had changed four decades later: Bill Clinton, who had Dylan sing a half-hearted "Chimes of Freedom" at his 1993 inaugural, had his Manhattan headquarters right down the street.

Before Dylan's racial journey dropped him off uptown, he had been the civil rights bard of the early 1960s, the converso who spent the years 1978 to 1987 accompanied by black female singers, and the minstrelsy-obsessed allegorist of the twenty-first century. Of course, it was typical, after Elvis, for white American pop singers to find their voices through someone else's blues, but Dylan's relationship to race is unique. Just three years earlier, he had named his 2001 album *"Love and Theft"* after Eric Lott's 1993 study of blackface minstrelsy, and in his film *Masked and Anonymous*, Dylan is visited by the specter of the blacked-up, banjo-playing Oscar Vogel (Ed Harris), taunting Dylan's character Jake Fate to remember the burnt cork origins of his musical identity. Rock and roll is filled with white imitators of black style, but none had contextualized the appropriation of black culture so inimitably. Dylan did not, like Van Morrison, completely lose his origins to sweet soul. He became a hybrid, hillbilly one minute, gospel singer the next. One thing's for sure: when Dylan opened his mouth to sing, he adopted many personae, but never that of a Minnesota Jew. (*Infidels*, his most Jewish album, has a kind of noir Zionism, with a range of emotions that includes neither kvetching nor kvelling.) He will never make a Klezmer album.[1] He was fond of Rimbaud's maxim, "Je est un autre," literally translated as "I is someone else," which could be a blues lyric. In his voice, Hank Williams and Woody Guthrie drifted in from the white working class, and Leadbelly and Robert Johnson as African American blues avatars. The former Robert Zimmerman spent a few years in Christianity, but all of his adult life, off and on, in a reckoning with blackness. "Nobody could sing the blues like Blind Willie McTell," he sang, but nobody sang about not being able to sing those blues like Dylan, which in its own way made for compelling blues.

By the year of his Apollo concert, Dylan had become a respected man of letters, nominated for a National Book Critics Circle Award and championed by Christopher Ricks for the Nobel Prize for Literature. And yet a purely textual reading would not explain how Robert Zimmerman of Hibbing, Minnesota, became the mongrel phenomenon of Bob Dylan through gospel shouting, blues wailing, and minstrel signifyin'. Like Huck Finn, Jay Gatsby, Al Jolson, and The White Negro, Bob Dylan is a creation based on an ethnic masquerade as old as the minstrel show. Dylan's venomous sneer has its origins in a particular form of racial mimesis that continues to draw millions of concertgoers, scrutinizing critics, and obsessive fans. As people sing along to imitate him, however, Dylan has become increasingly conscious of his ethnic imitations in general and his indebtedness to black bluesmen and divas in particular. What began as youthful imitation turned into impassioned activism and eventually racial ventriloquism. He saw through the fake appropriations and wanted to get to blackness as deeply as possible. In his journey from civil rights to minstrelsy, politics became sex, religion, and, finally, a way to come to terms with mortality and masks. The various iconic personae fashioned by Bob Dylan would not be possible without black America, and his work—blues, civil rights anthems, gospel songs, and more—repeatedly acknowledged this fact.

But did black America need Bob Dylan? Would he pass his audition for "Showtime at the Apollo"? He was performing at a fundraiser supporting Jazz at Lincoln Center, playing two songs with a septet led by Wynton Marsalis, the institution's artistic director, jazz's impassioned musical ambassador and biggest living celebrity. One of the music's most accomplished trumpet players (a Grammy winner in both jazz and classical) and beguiling raconteurs, he was the first jazz composer to win a Pulitzer Prize. His detractors have called him a "neoconservative" for his rejection of most music after the middle period of John Coltrane—including post–Ornette Coleman free jazz and anything with a whiff of rock or rap—yet in the service of funding the orchestra's new headquarters, which would open that fall at Columbus Circle in Manhattan, he was collaborating with pop stars Stevie Wonder, Paul Simon, and, on this night, Bob Dylan. Dylan apparently acted like quite the rock star during rehearsals, filling the room with expensive guitars that he didn't even touch. But before the show, the audience could hear him backstage riffing on his harmonica, sounding like he could have been around the corner on Lenox Avenue playing for spare change.

Jazz was not completely unfamiliar territory for Dylan. Jazz bassist Art Davis sat in on "Rocks and Gravel," an unreleased track from the *Freewheelin' Bob Dylan* sessions in 1963, when he was also the bass player for the John Coltrane Quartet. In *Chronicles, Vol. 1*, Dylan wrote of jamming with the avant-garde virtuoso Cecil Taylor ("Cecil could play regular piano if he wanted to"), as well as Don Cherry and Billy Higgins (in the years when they were blazing the new territory of free jazz alongside Ornette Coleman). In this remarkable passage from his memoir, he recalled crashing a rehearsal with Thelonious Monk: "I dropped in there once in the afternoon, just to listen—told him that I played folk music up the street. 'We all play folk music,' he said. Monk was in his own dynamic music even when he dawdled around."[2] This exchange resonated enough with Dylan to merit repeating four decades later, but even if he was curious enough to listen in, and even as he was hip to Monk's assertion that all music was folk music, he also admitted, "I liked modern jazz a lot, liked to listen to it in the clubs . . . but I didn't follow it and I wasn't caught up in it. There weren't ordinary words with specific meanings, and I needed to hear things plain and simple in the King's English, and folk songs are what spoke to me most directly" (94–95).

"We all play folk music": what a rich description of two musical rivers that diverged yet are fed by similar sources, both still driven to transform vernacular material into something new and strange. A black genius in a porkpie hat sent a powerful message to the scruffy Jewish kid that day, something that Dylan pondered for decades. In a scene from *Dont Look Back*, Dylan and Bob Neuwirth are facetiously snapping their fingers to a jazz recording, and while it may appear they are parodying the music, the pretentious hipsters are the real targets. In this passage, Dylan could admit his affection and curiosity while also pleading ignorance. Even if he claimed to prefer "the King's English," his use of it was hardly plain and simple. The author of "my warehouse eyes / My Arabian drums" could be abstract, associative, and dense, but his musical world was simple: variations on folk forms and the twelve-bar blues.

Blues was the turf where Dylan and Marsalis could meet. Marsalis's jazz canon was centered on Duke Ellington, Louis Armstrong, and Charlie Parker (all of whom would surface on Dylan's XM Radio show), and the blues flowed through it all. Marsalis's fundraiser was Dylan's second gig at the Apollo that year. In April he had performed a rage-against-the-dying-of-the-light rendition of Sam Cooke's civil rights anthem "A Change Is Gonna Come," a song Cooke wrote after he heard "Blowin' in the Wind" and thought, "Geez. A white boy writing a song like that?" Cooke would be gunned down a year after recording the song, and Dylan sang it like he was fighting for his life, ripping up his larynx to get the story out. On this June night, the circle closed even more. But before he could hit the stage, comedian Cedric the Entertainer, who was emceeing the event reading patter from a teleprompter, had to give him a hazing, testing the waters uptown. This was not Dylan's crowd. Lou

Reed's lyrics would have resonated: "Hey, white boy. What you doin' uptown?" The moment before a performer appears onstage is always sensitive, and for Dylan, who according to legend inspired Robbie Robertson to write "Stage Fright," this is especially the case. Cedric the Entertainer's introduction was more like a celebrity roast:

> Now, when you think of jazz and you think of the Apollo theater, there is one man that instantly comes to mind: Bob Dylan. [This gets a big laugh.] I don't know about y'all, but it just adds up to me. Jazz, Apollo, Bob Dylan. Could be my fuzzy math. Okay, it might seem like a stretch. Aiight. But when it comes to compelling songs that resonate profoundly today, here's what comes to my mind: How many cannonballs must fly before they are forever banned? The answer, my friend is blowin' in the wind. Now, the artist that wrote that song decades ago is not known as a jazz artist, but his body of work reflects something akin to jazz: change and adaptability. How else would you describe someone whose work has spanned four decades and collaborations with everyone from Willie Nelson to Beatle George Harrison? And, of course, he's received Grammys and lifetime achievement awards galore, all richly deserved. That achievement began with the spirit of rebellion that filled the jazz and folk clubs of the fifties and sixties. Many artists have come a long way since then, but few have truly been trailblazers. Ladies and gentlemen, would you please welcome Mr. Bob Dylan?

There were waves of applause, some of it polite, some baffled, and some thunderous, especially from the Dylan fans among those paying for four-figure tickets or on press comps. The band began playing a B-flat blues at a snail's pace, complete with Ellingtonian splashes of brass and a lilting piano riff. It was a blues that sounded wounded yet wrapped in elegance. Then a low, gravelly voice ascended from the crypt: "Well I ride on a mail train, baby . . . Can't buy uh-ah thrill," Dylan rasped. The horns answered his call with taunts, and he would often turn around in a mixture of disbelief and simpatico bliss. *Highway 61 Revisited* and the brash young man who first delivered those lines had receded in the rear-view mirror decades earlier. "It Takes a Lot to Laugh, It Takes a Train to Cry." This cryptic title was now making more sense. The more you travel, the deeper your emotions, and Dylan was singing a traveling blues. "Don't say I never warned you / When your train gets lost," he snarled, and he seemed in danger of getting lost himself, but the band managed to catch up with him, rushing to the next bar and reining him in. The blues found him in the end. Marsalis was laying down the iron law of swing, and it did not work against Dylan but pushed him into a groove where he had never gone. Raising his voice just above the cellar for emphasis, Dylan rasped, "I tried to tell everybody, but I could not get across."

The next song, "Don't Think Twice, It's Alright," tried to get something else across. A devastating breakup tune dating back to *Freewheelin'*, Dylan stayed nestled in the nether regions of what was left of his range. Marsalis's arrangement was so dense, it seemed impenetrable, but Dylan attempted to croon his way in anyway. Drummer Herlin Riley rumbled a Latin groove known as "The Big Four" (bomp-ca-bomp-ca-bom-CHA). Marsalis played lines behind Dylan, circling around the melody, finding rhythmic and harmonic counterpoints that strayed way beyond the song's simple origins. Dylan was so startled he lost his place in a song he had been singing since 1963, singing the line "on the dark side of the road" twice, but it hardly mattered. It was his "jazz singer" moment: he was looking into the mirror and realizing the man on the other side understood his music better than he did. He was in sync, finally sitting in with a real jazz band, perhaps as he had wanted to when he crashed Monk's rehearsal all those years earlier. As the band slowly quieted down on the out chorus, Dylan's harmonica lines were fading out, too. Dylan seemed shaken when it was over. He nearly tripped over his microphone. (And this is someone used to microphones.) But he and Marsalis shook hands. The two songs had ended in a musical draw.

When Blackness Was a Virtue

Dylan had reason to be shaken. The septet had recognized things in him that he seemed afraid yet exhilarated to find reflected back from musicians of such intimidating authority. They were also, however, channeling a deeper identity narrative for him, one that Dylan was still playing out that summer night on 125th Street. He had great reverence for this tradition and perhaps felt unworthy as well. The Apollo Theater performance was a replay of a four-decade run of fame that had included teenage appropriation, youthful activism, and half a lifetime of finding his musical voice through someone else's blues. It began when he was a teenager and traded in his electric guitar for an acoustic after an Odetta record stopped him dead in his tracks. After he soaked up her strumming and singing style, he performed for her during his brief stint as a matriculated derelict student at the University of Minnesota, and her encouragement helped give him the confidence to make that fateful journey to New York City during that cold, auspicious winter of 1961. Soon after he arrived, he played harmonica with Harry Belafonte's version of "Midnight Special" for his first record date; the musicians on the session laughed at Dylan's nervous attempts to keep the rhythm by thudding his foot so loudly that it caused reverb throughout the studio.

Authenticity was the rage in a folk scene dominated by white college kids and dropouts affecting the voices of the Delta and the

Dust Bowl. Rock and roll was also a white, adolescent affectation of the sounds of blackness and the working class, but the fashion on the Greenwich Village folk scene called for musicians to chase not merely style or profit (although there would be plenty of that for a few of them) but political and social change. It was Dylan's bohemian girlfriend, Suze Rotolo (she is on his arm on the *Freewheelin'* *Bob Dylan* cover), who got him involved with CORE (Congress of Racial Equality). He began writing songs about Emmett Till, Hattie Carroll, and James Meredith and crafting words that would be belted out at the March on Washington by Peter, Paul, and Mary: "How many years can some people exist until they're allowed to be free."

Yet Dylan's time in the trenches of the civil rights movement coincided with a notable absence of the black musical influence he absorbed elsewhere. When he confronted the struggle face to face in civil rights demonstrations, he did not sing in the blues-inflected drawl of his 1961 performances of Bukka White's "Fixin' To Die" or Blind Lemon Jefferson's "See That My Grave Is Kept Clean" (both featured on his first album, though not staples of his live sets at the time). Instead he stuck to Okie affectations. Consciously or unconsciously, Dylan seemed to sense that this was not an occasion for musical blackface. He also recorded two blues standards for the *Freewheelin'* sessions—Big Joe Williams's "Baby Please Don't Go" and Robert Johnson's "Milk Cow's Calf's Blues"—but left them off the final album. Even though he sang, in "With God on Our Side," "The country I come from is called the Midwest," his phrasing evoked an imaginary region inspired by his teenage readings of Guthrie's *Bound for Glory* or John Steinbeck's *Grapes of Wrath*. That twang—not anything resembling his blues invocations—was on display in his two most memorable political appearances, both during the incendiary summer of 1963. Whatever region he invoked, artifice was all. In footage from his performance in a Greenwood, Mississippi, cotton field, Dylan is surrounded by black men in sunglasses, sweating under a work shirt and belting out "Only a Pawn in Their Game," a screed about the assassination of Medgar Evers written weeks earlier:

And the Negro's name
Is used it is plain
For the politician's gain
As he rises to fame

He sings these lines like he sprang right out of the Dust Bowl. The Negro's name may be used for the politician's gain, but the bluesman's cadences are noticeably absent from Dylan's delivery; he would not make civil rights appearances as Norman Mailer's White Negro. Dylan was not playing the hipster contemplating existential dread. He looked like a humble singer-activist, earnestly intoning his finger-pointing invective in that sultry cotton field, and he was not about to channel his inner Robert Johnson while he was deep in the Delta. Theo Bikel, who brought Dylan down along with Pete Seeger, recalled, "Bob said that he hadn't met a colored person until he was nine years old and apologized that he had so little to offer" (Shelton 1986, 179).

Dylan also avoided racial affectations at the March on Washington, where he sang "When the Ship Comes In" with Joan Baez warbling by his side (she had dragged him to the event) and, repeating his Mississippi cotton field performance, "Only a Pawn in Their Game." He was apparently inspired to write "When the Ship Comes In" after being denied a hotel room with Baez and recalling a performance of Bertolt Brecht's "Pirate Jenny." The words he summoned, "The whole wide world is watchin'," were fortuitous. "The greatness of works of art lies solely in their power to let those things be heard which ideology conceals," wrote Theodor Adorno ("Lyric Poetry and Society," 58). Dylan was revealing all, yet his performance was met with a dismissal in the *New York Times* and some ironic asides from comedian Dick Gregory. Yet he was singing into a momentous podium. He belted these anthems to a crowd of 250,000 as a warm-up act for Martin Luther King's "I Have a Dream" speech. This was during Dylan's brief (albeit glorious) period of political engagement. When he sang about lynchings and assassinations, he was joining the movement, but in this period and in these performances, he avoided phrasing out of African American vernacular. It would have been an untoward imitation.

Just a few months later, on December 16, 1963, Dylan made a drunken acceptance speech for the Tom Paine Award from the National Emergency Civil Liberties Committee in which he attempted to bite the hand that fed him, expressing sympathy for Lee Harvey Oswald weeks after the Kennedy assassination and saying this about his appearance on the Washington mall: "I was on the March on Washington up on the platform and I looked around at all the Negroes there and I didn't see any Negroes that looked like none of my friends. My friends don't wear *suits*. My friends don't have to wear any kind of thing to prove that they're respectable Negroes" (Shelton 1986, 201). He clearly felt ill at ease with what seemed like a bourgeois costume for a radical event. In the 2000 interview that appeared in Martin Scorsese's *No Direction Home*, he would reflect that he was standing a few feet away from King when he made his speech—it had "a profound effect on me to this day," he recalled—but at the time, he was also pledging a political *non serviam*. He had looked at blackness from the outside and clearly wanted in. When he was speaking irreverently about the March and spoke of his friends who wore more casual clothes, he was claiming a kinship of another kind. "I'm not part of no Movement," he told Nat Hentoff in 1964. "If I was, I wouldn't be able to do anything else but be in 'the Movement.' I just can't make it with any organization."

On *Another Side of Bob Dylan*, recorded in one Beaujolais-soaked evening in 1964, Dylan bid fare-thee-well to politics. "I was so much older then, I'm younger than that now," he sang in a voice that no longer invoked Woody Guthrie. But his fixation on black culture—now removed from the label of "protest songs" that he always protested—turned more playful and, in the case of "Spanish Harlem Incident," erotic. Dylan's racial crossover was not only musical and political but, at various times in his life, religious and sexual. The song is addressed to a "Gypsy gal" with "pearly eyes" and "flashing diamond teeth," a reference to old-school bling, possibly to the blues singer "Diamond Teeth" Mary—certainly to her dental style and what its extravagance signified in African American communities. This gypsy gal represents an ideal of sensuality that makes him disparage his own whiteness: "The night is pitch black, come an' make my / Pale face fit into place, ah, please!" When Dylan sings these lines, he is gazing longingly at blackness but not trying to imitate it. In these images, he attempts, earnestly and somewhat awkwardly, to match his lover's dark skin with the night. At the song's end, he begs the Gypsy gal to "surround" him so that he can determine whether he's "really real." After Dylan distanced himself from politics, in this song, he brought himself closer to interracial Eros and his eventual redefinition of his musical identity in terms of the black female diva. A year later, in "From a Buick 6," he would playfully sing about a "soulful mama" who "keeps me hid," a lover who "walks like Bo Diddley / And she don't need no crutch," indicating that it takes a black rhythm-and-blues guitarist to truly walk the walk. The lover of "Spanish Harlem Incident" also needs no assistance. There were many associations swirling in Dylan's head during the songwriting binge that included "Spanish Harlem Incident" as a charming but minor track in a harvest that also included the far more monumental "To Ramona," "Chimes of Freedom," and "Mr. Tambourine Man." As the title suggested, *Another Side of Bob Dylan* meant to show that Dylan was revealing a new aspect of his complicated persona, embarking on a post-political identity that included sharing a momentous joint with the Beatles, a breakup with Suze Rotolo, and a halfhearted tribute to his fling with Joan Baez. "It ain't me, babe," he sang on the album's closing track.

But who was he? Never before had Dylan sounded so unaffected; the Guthrie-inspired twang was gone, and he sounded like he was itching for a rock-and-roll band behind him, which he would soon get. There were black musicians in his orbit, and he never believed, as he sang in "Chimes of Freedom," in the "lies that life [was] black and white." He was working (without much satisfaction) with the producer Tom Wilson, the first black man to rise up in the world of pop production, who had previously produced Cecil Taylor's *Jazz Advance* (1955) and Sun Ra's *Futuristic Sounds of Sun Ra* (1961). Wilson was a jazz partisan who thought folk music was just for "dumb guys" until he heard Dylan's lyrics; "Mr. Tambourine Man" was inspired by the giant tambourine of the black guitarist Bruce Langhorne, who himself did not learn about the inspiration until he read Dylan's interview in the *Biograph* liner notes in 1985.[3] Stevie Wonder, Sam Cooke, and even Duke Ellington were all covering "Blowin' in the Wind." Dylan had distanced himself from politics in the year of the Freedom Summer, but in "Spanish Harlem Incident" he sang about his desire to become one with blackness in a different way.

Yet he also knew the price of artifice, and the anger he would express about racial injustice would also be directed toward racial affectation in one of his greatest songs. When Dylan entered Columbia's Studio A on June 15, 1965, to record "Like a Rolling Stone," he gave the following order to guitarist Mike Bloomfield: "I don't want you to play any of that B. B. King shit. I don't want you to play any of the fucking blues." This was a strange directive for a guitarist who had played with the Paul Butterfield Blues Band— someone who had played nothing *but* the fucking blues. That "something else" was a simple 1–4–5 riff, which Dylan had said was inspired by Richie Valens's 1958 "La Bamba." "Like a Rolling Stone" is a jeremiad against artifice, lashing out at Miss Lonely, a female poseur who affects what Muddy Waters embodied for real. The song explodes with fury, but it's never been clear exactly who its target is. Speculations have ranged from Edie Sedgwick in particular to his audience in general, with more than a modicum of misogyny in the former case, misanthropy in the latter.

"I'm a rollin' stone," intoned Waters, and Hank Williams wasn't ashamed of identifying himself that way either. (In D. A. Pennebaker's *Dont Look Back*, filmed shortly before the song was written, Dylan is caught backstage playing Williams's "Lost Highway" with its "I'm a rolling stone" lyric.) Miss Lonely graduated from "the finest school all right," but no one ever taught her how to "live out on the street." Like many a white college student in 1965, she might have fetishized an old bluesman like Waters—she may have listened to him at Newport or on a record in her dorm—but if she tried to live like him, it would have been a temporary bit of slumming. For Dylan, authenticity was not a fetish. Yet what seems to put her truly beneath contempt, what makes her most worthy of his scorn, is not that she ignored all those warnings that this doll was bound to fall, but that she is a Bob Dylan fan. "You used to be so amused / At Napoleon in rags and the language that he used"; "You said you'd never compromise / With the mystery tramp, but now you realize / He's not selling any alibis / As you stare into the vacuum of his eyes / And ask him do you want to make a deal?" Dylan is the mystery tramp, the Napoleon in rags who used language so cunningly, and he is berating Miss Lonely for following him without really understanding him, while he also takes aim at himself. To be *like* a rolling stone is to be a pretender to the throne of Hank Williams and Muddy Waters. How does it feel to affect the styles of those less privileged than you? How does it feel to be ersatz? The voice that snarls it triumphs in identifying a bohemian who has the style but not the credibility—who can't walk the walk. This masterpiece of bile remains a crowd pleaser. But is it in the voice of the Dylan who wants the gypsy gal of "Spanish Harlem Incident" to make him "really real," or does it revel in its artificiality, its invented persona of the mystery tramp? The mystery of the mystery tramp continued to confound.

There is a film of Waters performing "Rolling Stone" at the Newport Folk Festival in 1960, entrancing an interracial crowd a few years before Dylan became the festival's star (in 1963 and 1964) and Judas (in 1965, when his version of the brand-new "Like a Rolling Stone" blew the eardrums off some folkie purists). No one had a problem with Muddy Waters playing electric there, and in his lyrics he took pride in his vagabond status. Being a rolling stone gave him strength, resilience, and something to sing about:

Well, my mother told my father,
just before hmmm, I was born,
"I got a boy child's comin',
He's gonna be, he's gonna be a rollin' stone"

This is in the song where men leave their heartbroken women behind and the singer wishes he were a catfish so that fine-looking women would fish after him. All this would be insufferable bragging were it not for Waters's ingenious guitar playing, seductive singing, and devastating stage presence. Waters's refrain about himself was a destiny first uttered by his parents: "He's gonna be a rolling stone." It is blues stoicism, affirmation, and defiant self-possession. He will gather no moss, endure, and sing about it in a thrilling performance to the white college kids at Newport in 1960. "Nothin' in ramblin'," sang Memphis Minnie, but Waters's song made it sound appealing. Dylan takes this trope, twists it, and throws it in the face of Miss Lonely, who was schooled (in the finest school, all right) for other things. Sitting out the civil rights movement in 1965 (once the bill was passed that he sang for in 1963), he looks toward Waters as the ultimate image of black masculinity and musical depth, an exemplar that Miss Lonely could never attain or understand. And yet there is something about the condition of identifying that phoniness that created a new hybrid genre: a six-minute pop song bursting at the seams with Beat poetry and surrealism, a song that made Dylan realize he should put aside his novel and other literary ambitions—because he could channel the range of his ideas and his ever-inspired revenge fantasies into a song, a "piece of vomit," as he described it. (Bob Neuwirth said the original draft of the song went on for pages. It would have taken up an entire side of a record.) But Dylan recognized it was no mere regurgitation. "Like a Rolling Stone" had a life of its own. Muddy Waters—the rolling stone himself—receded into the distance.

"Pops, I Want to Marry Mavis"

Dylan still belts out "Like a Rolling Stone" in encores about a hundred times a year. Apart from the period when he eliminated all secular material from his set in 1979–80, it has been a staple of his tours since 1965 and 1966. But there was one performance where he did not get the last word. In a 1992 appearance for the tenth anniversary of the *David Letterman Show*, Dylan sang the song in a perfunctory nasal growl, and it is only in the final choruses when the gospel legend Mavis Staples, leading an all-star chorus of backup singers that also included Michelle Shocked, Roseanne Cash, Nancy Griffith, and Emmylou Harris, kicked new life into the song. "Tell me, ohhhh . . . how does it feeee-huuul . . ." she wailed, growing more forceful with every verse. She flashed knowing looks to Dylan. The question "How does it feel?" gained a new authority as a spiritual invocation from a virtuoso gospel diva. The performance was a reminder of how Staples could powerfully steal the show from a rock star, as she did in the Staples' incendiary duet on The Band's "The Weight" in Martin Scorsese's *Last Waltz*. She was both a rival and love interest as well as a model for the musical self Dylan wanted to be—an erotic and creative nexus that would appear increasingly in his work in the next few years and play into his artistic redefinition.

Staples was the youngest daughter in the Staple Singers, a gospel dynasty that scored crossover hits with pop covers, including Dylan's "The Times They Are a-Changin'" and "Masters of War." "This was inspirational music," Staples said, and she made it sound that way, bringing out the blues, melisma, and sophisticated cadences of the gospel church, bringing the music all back home in a different way. When Dylan met the Staple Singers in 1962, they were unfamiliar with his work, but he knew theirs up and down. He quoted verses from "Sit Down Servant" to them, and demonstrating his deep knowledge of their recordings, said, "Pops, you have this — velvet voice and Mavis, you have this big, robust voice." He was smitten with more than just her voice. "Pops, I want to marry Mavis," Dylan said on film, and, contrary to his biographies, he wasn't joking. He actually did ask her to marry him. Staples recalled, "We courted for about seven years, and it was my fault that we didn't go on and get married." Staples said she believed that Dr. King wanted her to "stay black," and it was a decision she would regret. (Dylan would later marry Sara Lownds instead.) Dylan and Staples did not go on to be the next Johnny Cash and June Carter, but the image of African American women would haunt his writing. "Outlaw Blues": "I got a woman in Jackson, / I ain't gonna say her name / She's a brown-skin woman, but I love her just the same"; and, in a lamentable image, "I Want You": "Well, I return to the Queen of Spades. . . ."

Around the time Dylan was writing this line, he was also typing out *Tarantula*, his only "novel," and while the book was abandoned and disowned by its author, and its random, associative passages do

not succeed as experimental prose, it does provide access to the
stream of consciousness rambling inside Dylan's head in 1966. That
was the year it all came crashing down, when his muse was operat-
ing at such a frenzied pace, what he couldn't document in the ex-
traordinary songs on the fifteen-month binge of brilliance that produced *Bringing It All Back Home, Highway 61 Revisited,* and *Blonde on
Blonde* ended up in prose effluvia under contract with Macmillan.
Among the many jokes, riffs, and half-baked images that float
around the book, the most constant trope is his worshipful images
of black women: "i am just a guitar player—with no absurd fears of
her reputation, Black Gal co-exists with melody & I want to feel my
evaporation like Black Gal feels her co-existence" (*Tarantula,* 115).
The narrator of *Tarantula,* like the singer of "Spanish Harlem Incident," merges sexual desire with an urge to get inside the meaning
of the blues, through an erotic "co-existence." The book's opening
line is "aretha / crystal jukebox of hymm and him." This is not
Aretha Franklin the real person but a dream of the archetypal Queen
of Soul, his idealized vision of what Miss Lonely is not. "aretha"
haunts the entire book. "My soulful mama, she keeps me hid,"
Dylan sang on "From a Buick 6," and the soulful mama of *Tarantula*
keeps the author shrouded as well. While never coherent, the book
is consistent in its sexualized images of mixing it up: "aretha-golden
sweet / whose nakedness is a piercing thing" (19), "in the winter a
blackface musician announces he is from Two Women" (57), "aretha
in the blues dunes" (61), "aretha faking her intestinal black soul
across all the fertile bubbles & whims & flashy winos" (62). Near
the end of the book, "bob dylan," a lowercase version of his invented persona of the moment, is pronounced dead: "Here lies bob
dylan / murdered / from behind / with trembling flesh" (101). But
his plans for a black female soul goddess are just beginning as the
book ends: "in new york she's known as just plain aretha . . . i shall
play her as my trump card" (115). "The Queen of Spades" from "I

Want You" is the Queen of Soul trump card of *Tarantula*. Between 1978 and 1987, in the studio, at church, in the concert halls, and in the bedroom, Dylan would lean on African American female singers as backups in all kinds of ways.

"White Brother"

From Odetta to the folk scene, civil rights to Judas, Mavis to "aretha": in five years, Robert Zimmerman had become the celebrity Bob Dylan, an icon imprisoned by his own fame. A few years after Dylan attempted to liberate his image of black female sexuality in attempting to write a novel, he also reentered the fray of political songs—a realm he had otherwise relinquished—for two scorching anthems in support of two black men in prison. He would have nothing to do with Woodstock Nation, but in 1971, a newspaper article about the shooting of Black Panther George Jackson, gunned down while trying to escape San Quentin, inspired a return to his protest mode of 1963. "Some of us are prisoners, the rest of us are guards," sang Dylan in the single "George Jackson." He was clearly identifying with the former, aligning himself with a violent, controversial radical figure at a time when he seemed politically complacent. (The song would never be issued on an album or performed live.) Four years later, he was among the celebrities sent copies of Hurricane Carter's prison memoir, *The Sixteenth Round*, which claimed that Carter had been framed by a racist judge and jury for a crime he didn't commit. There has been much debate about Carter's claim, but Dylan put himself on a mission as a kind of identification: "The first time I saw him, I left knowing one thing . . . I realized that the man's philosophy and my philosophy were running down the same road, and you don't meet too many people like that." Dylan did not simply don black causes like a pair of Miss Lonely's earrings; he identified with the story and the man, although once some of the facts about Carter came out, he may have thought twice. He has not performed the song live since 1976.

In his film *Renaldo and Clara*, a sprawling, improvised account of the Rolling Thunder Revue, there is a section where Dylan is outside the Apollo Theater in Harlem, three decades before his duet with Wynton Marsalis. As a roving reporter, unknown as celebrity Bob Dylan, he asks a group of African American locals on 125th Street about the Carter case and, interspersed with a rehearsal take from the song, they all avow his innocence. (For contrast there is an interview with a seventy-two-year-old white cop, who tells Dylan he's afraid to express his opinion.) The line it is drawn, and Dylan, called a "white brother" by Carter, comes down on the boxer's side. When Dylan played a benefit for Carter at Rahway Penitentiary in New Jersey, a photo-op was staged for *People* magazine. Dylan was wearing whiteface, which he wore throughout the tour as part of the commedia dell'arte ambience, and also, he said, "so the audience could see me." Here he turns minstrelsy inside out, reversing the poles of significance and showing the artificiality of the social constructs of race. Carter is behind a cage (brought in for the shoot) in shadow, beaming in Dylan's presence. Dylan is looking in, fascinated, driven, a painted vision of artificial whiteness. He would soon find a way into blackness that would involve gospel harmonies and, ultimately, what that gospel music was all about.

The Queens of Rhythm

Difficult years followed the triumphs of Rolling Thunder Revue. Once he washed off his whiteface makeup, Bob Dylan had a very public midlife crisis. He had just gotten divorced, was feeling increasingly uncertain on stage, and was having religious visions. To subsidize his multimillion-dollar divorce, he began what became known as his "alimony tour," barnstorming 110 cities in ten countries and commercializing his repertoire with disco arrangements and Neil Diamond–style jumpsuits. Some men get a sports car or a mistress; Bob Dylan hired a group of African American backup singers. He appreciated their glitz and decoration, but they were there also to prove something about his artistic and sexual prowess. "When I got divorced," Dylan said, "I really got divorced." Guitarist Billy Cross recalled that the costumes made the band look like a "large aggregation of pimps," and the singers, ostensibly hired for their gospel cadences, felt a little tarted up. Debi Dye-Gibson, part of the original lineup, recalled, "We looked like hookers. I felt a little stupid singing 'Blowin' in the Wind' with my boobs hanging out." On *Live at Budokan*, recorded near the beginning of the tour, the song "Oh, Sister," from 1975's *Desire*, is transformed from a foreshadowing of religious conversion to a funk-based session of traded moans and groans with his backup singers. "I happen to be one of the supremes," Dylan wrote in the liner notes to *Bringing It All Back Home*, and what seemed like a surrealist non sequitur in 1965 became a declaration of intent. The Queens of Rhythm, as Dylan would later reverentially dub his backup singers, seemed, like the rest of his 1978 incarnation, to be so much ersatz accoutrements. But the story of how Dylan got his groove back by becoming his own soul sister is also a distinctly American narrative of racial appropriation and sexual exploitation, of selling out, getting saved, and owning up.

Street-Legal (1978) was the sonic result of what divorce proceedings, screeching, shouting, the coked-out Rolling Thunder Revue, and plumbing the muse could do to Dylan, who had done everything possible to make his voice sound heavier and more ravaged than his mere thirty-seven years would seem to have made possible. He had been writing songs (never released) with Helena Springs, one of his backup singers and new girlfriend. Robert Christgau would dub the singers the "Dylanettes," after Ray Charles's Raelettes, who secularized the call and response of the gospel church, a soulful mixture of blasphemy and musical genius that made it all the way to the top of the charts. A soulful female chorus accompanied Dylan on tracks from *New Morning* (1971), which came with a back cover of a baby-faced Dylan from 1961 standing shyly and reverentially next to African American blues singer Victoria Spivey, with whom he played harmonica on an early record date. But while "Father of Night" and "The Man in Me" were adorned with a female trio's oohs and aahs, it wasn't until *Street-Legal* and the alimony tour that Dylan finally realized all those obsessive references by having a chorus to talk back to him. "The Changing of the Guards" is cryptic even by Dylan's standards, but the Dylanettes respond to the end of every phrase, for emphasis, drama, a gospel echo chamber: "The captain waits above the celebration / Sending his thoughts to a beloved maid / Whose ebony face is beyond communication." As Dylan sings of a captain in love with an ebony-faced maid, the quartet of Dylanettes sing "ebony face" back at Dylan, adding clarity and emphasis to an opaque song, which ends with "a pale ghost retreating." They repeat the end of every phrase, and continue the sass no matter how perplexing the lines. Dylan is the captain of the tour and the record, but the dialectic gets reversed.

"New Pony," the second song, is more direct. On his way to religious conversion, Dylan is first having an immersion in a blues-based celebration of carnal pleasure, one that, in his version, is expressed in the call and response with a chorus that included his current girlfriend and future wife. "How much longer?" they would sing, repeatedly, like a gospel mantra, while Dylan, basing his blues on a Son House standard, is no longer at arm's length from his source material. He is not decorating it with surrealism or Beat poetry, French symbolism, Brecht, or modernism. The guards have changed. "I had a pony / Her name was Lucifer," he sings, foreshadowing the religious conversion to come but meanwhile celebrating raunchy, forbidden pleasures with an allusion to a familiar character in blues lyrics. There is conviction in his voice. Unlike his earlier blues, like the gorgeously warped "Pledging My Time" on *Blonde on Blonde*, he sounds less removed than ever from the genre he plunders. "You're so nasty and you're so bad / But I swear, I love you, yes I do," he sings, goaded on by the chants of "how much longer?"

By the end of the tour, the struggle that had begun as a sexual obsession and musical immersion ended in religious conversion. By the time he announced that "Christ is real," he was even further away from the Hibbing bar mitzvah boy he had long been trying to leave behind. *Newsweek* caught him in 1963 lying about his name, his upbringing, and putting Abe and Beatty Zimmerman up in a hotel, filled with nacchus to see their Robert play at Carnegie Hall. "Never so utterly fake," pronounced Greil Marcus in his *Rolling Stone* review of *Street-Legal*, but even under the murky production and Vegas staging, Dylan was trying to get away from the thing he railed against in "Like a Rolling Stone." Charlie Patton's lyrics to "Pony Blues" were already blatant, raw, and racialized: "Well saddle my pony, saddle up my black mare / Baby, saddle my pony, saddle up my black mare." In Dylan's arrangement, modeled on Son House's cover of Patton, he makes a similar entreaty: "Come over here, pony / I wanna ride one time up on you." Dylan is no longer raging against Miss Lonely, who could never be an actual rolling stone. He is fusing his sexual desire with his artistic and ethnic aspirations. On "New Pony," with Helena Springs in tow, he tried to channel his inner Son House, to find credibility through sex, drugs, racial appropriation, and, eventually, the Bible.

Although Dylan offered many explanations for why he became a Christian—including a cross thrown on stage by a fan during the alimony tour and an encounter with Jesus in a Tucson hotel room—Springs pointed to a conversation with Dylan in which she asked him, "Do you ever pray?" He eventually did, producing a trio of

Christian albums—*Slow Train Coming* (1979), *Saved* (1980), and, in part, *Shot of Love* (1981)—that preached the word of God with soul inflections. "You gotta serve somebody," he sang on his first Grammy Award–winning single, sounding a little like an adenoidal Al Green. The song would go down in the disco with a message for the prayer meeting, while he is goaded on by the chorus of Dylanettes repeating "serve somebody." He was, he sang, the property of Jesus, but his heart still belonged to backup muses. A line from the title track of *Slow Train Coming* suggested a spiritual sequel to "New Pony": "I had a woman down in Alabama, / She was a backwoods girl, but she sure was realistic," he sang in the Alabama recording studio. "Don't wanna be with nobody tonight / Veronica not here, Mavis just ain't right," he sang on the title track of *Shot of Love* (1981). The shot of love was a spiritual injection, but his paradigm for fulfillment was still summed up by the name "Mavis." By 1986, he had christened the chorus the Queens of Rhythm. One of his backup singers, Carolyn Dennis, became his secret wife and gave birth to a daughter, Desiree. Another, Madelyn Quebec, was his secret mother-in-law. Dylan would often jokingly introduce the singers as, "My ex-wife, my next wife, my girlfriend, and my fiancée." This was not exactly hyperbole. On his way to finding Jesus, Dylan worshiped at the shrine of the black female voice, and his queens were his lovers, sirens, and surrogate divas. Back in 1966, Dylan's "I Want You" foreshadowed the Queens of Rhythm with racial syntax that does not age particularly well: "Well, I return to the Queen of Spades / And talk with my chambermaid. / She knows that I'm not afraid / To look at her." Twenty years later, Dylan is not afraid to look at his Queens of Rhythm, but is he afraid to truly give them voice?

This question comes to the fore in a performance in New Zealand in February 1986, with Dylan backed by Tom Petty and the Heartbreakers and the Queens of Rhythm: Queen Esther Marrow, Madelyn Quebec, Elisecia Wright, and Debra Byrd.[4] Absent from the lineup is Carolyn Dennis, who had given birth to Dylan's fifth child, Desiree Dennis-Dylan, three days earlier. But Dennis's mother, Madelyn Quebec, is present, leading the melisma and flashing many a stern look. Quebec was also one of Dylan's lovers and a member of the Raelettes, Ray Charles's backup singers. The birth of Desiree and Dylan's subsequent marriage to Dennis were well-kept secrets for fifteen years, until the publication of Howard Sounes's *Down the Highway* in 2001. But Quebec's disapproving look speaks volumes, and just as Dylan kept his new wife and child on the down low, he also appears to have imposed a gag order on the Queens of Rhythm. Ray Charles caused a scandalous revolution by engaging in gospel-style call and response with his Raelettes. They would sing "Hit the Road, Jack" and Charles would reply, "What you say?" Even songs by white rockers, like the Who's "My Generation," engaged in such dialogic antiphonal exchanges. But Dylan is not interested in what the Queens of Rhythm have to say. They are there to pad and amplify his attenuated and increasingly uncertain voice, more Echo and Narcissus than call and response.

In the February 1986 performance, however, the Queens of Rhythm will have none of it. The song they sing is "In the Garden," Dylan's most-performed song of his gospel period. It is built on a series of questions about whether the people who crucified Christ knew who they were dealing with. The Queens of Rhythm don't answer the questions, but they do overpower his delivery of them. "Did they speak out against him, did they dare?" Dylan asks. The Queens of Rhythm do dare to speak out and rebel against this gag rule, overthrowing their king and musically forcing him to listen to their dissenting wails. He eventually gives up and lets them finish the line, simply groaning, "Aaaaaaaaaaah."

Dylan would later admit that he hid behind the Queens of Rhythm, believing that the crowd would pay more attention to them than to him, to compensate for his own musical uncertainty. "I had them up there so I wouldn't feel so bad," he said. This was not a good trade for many critics. "May Bobby never indenture soul sisters again," Robert Christgau wrote of *Saved*, where "In the Garden" first appeared. But for Dylan, the position of the Queens of Rhythm was more prominent than indentured servitude. They prayed with him before every concert, fed him soul food, filled in his phrases, and shared his bed; at least one of them gave birth to his child and was willing to be his clandestine wife. Dylan's born-again Christian phase lasted only a few years, but his ethnic conversion was just beginning. He was no mere White Negro, taking on the sounds of blackness without the burdens. He was closer to Mezz Mezzrow, the hipster freakshow of the 1946 book *Really the Blues*, a Jewish musician who believed he was physically turning black. Dylan was finding Jesus through the gospel singers, and the internalization altered his intonations, not only in song, but even in speech. He was no longer the Oakie-inflected bard of civil rights but a prematurely aged bluesman. He would eventually cast Christianity aside, but once he went black, he never went back.

Dylan would later say that the period of the February 1986 concert was the lowest creative ebb of his career. In the 1980s, his most erratic musical decade, Dylan was at his most inspired when guided by the muse of racial guilt. In "Blind Willie McTell," a powerful song that Dylan perversely left off *Infidels* in 1983, he stood in deference to the blues master of the song's title, venerating McTell's authenticity in contrast to his glammed-up Queens of Rhythm—and ultimately his own artifice: "Them charcoal gypsy maidens / Can strut their feathers well / But nobody can sing the blues / Like Blind Willie McTell." Charcoal, like burnt cork, was commonly used by white minstrel performers blacking themselves up. Dylan's use of "charcoal" suggests that he is singing not only about actual black women wearing ruffled feathers, but perhaps also about singers imitating and appropriating the blues that, in Dylan's thinking, McTell does better than anyone else. He is surely aware that authenticity is a fetish, but as with Potter Stewart's definition of pornography, he knows it when he hears it. "Blind Willie McTell" is a musical mea culpa that saw the light of day only because it had been out on the street anyway. Dylan had searched for salvation through African American vernacular and was returning with a wearied response. On the song, while singing about being unworthy, he nonetheless creates a stunning portrait of plantations, whips, "the ghost of slavery ships," and the rock star's plundering. He was paying respect and laying down his own weary tune, a complicated story about how the blues can be translated all the way from New Orleans to Jerusalem and back again. The song is based on the haunting descending chords of "St. James Infirmary Blues," a song about Eros, mourning, and melancholia, looking on a dead lover's corpse in an age of syphilis, inimitably rendered in Louis Armstrong's 1928 recording. "I'm staring out the window of the St. James Hotel / And I know no one can sing the blues like Blind Willie McTell," Dylan sang, acknowledging his cultural debt. The St. James Hotel is a place where a rock star can hang his hat for the night before playing a stadium gig, a temporary resting place. McTell's blues are forever.

Three years later, in "Brownsville Girl," the Queens of Rhythm purr, croon, and map the dramatic action of a song in search of something real in a world gone wrong, or at least a world where the stars have been torn down. "Now I know she ain't you but she's here and she's got that dark rhythm in her soul," he sings, essentializing the hell out of his clandestine wife while she provides soulful sustenance in the background. And yet he gives way to the Queens' voices. He sings, "Hang on to me, baby, and let's hope that the roof stays on," and they scream in response. The Queens of Rhythm helped him get righteous until he could strike through the mask himself, owning up to the racial hybrid he was striving to be all along.

"Brownsville Girl" was a high point in an otherwise fallow period. In *Chronicles, Vol. 1* he recalls taking a break from a listless rehearsal with the Grateful Dead in California in 1987, the year after "Brownsville Girl," and wandering off to a jazz dive where an old black singer got under his skin. "The singer reminded me of Billy Eckstine," Dylan writes. "He wasn't very forceful, but he didn't have to be; he was relaxed, but he sang with natural power. Suddenly and without warning, it was like the guy had an open window to my soul. It was like he was saying, 'You should do it this way.'" Dylan had a revelation that he didn't need to strain to hit notes coming from a younger man's angst with a voice long eviscerated by nicotine and howling. Later that year, his mystical encounters with black vocalists continued when he realized, on a foggy night in Switzerland, that he could deliver himself what the Queens of Rhythm had been providing for him: "It's almost like I heard a voice. It wasn't like it was even me thinking it. *I'm determined to stand whether God will deliver me or not.* And all of a sudden everything just exploded. It exploded every which way. And I noticed that all the people out there—I was used to them looking at the girl singers, they were good-looking girls, you know? And like I say, I had them up there so I wouldn't feel so bad. But when that happened, nobody was looking at the girls anymore. They were looking at the main mike. And that is when I sort of knew: I've got to go out and play these songs. That's just what I must do."

Once Dylan found his inner soul sister, the Queens of Rhythm lost a gig.

The High Muddy Waters

Although he did not work with the Queens of Rhythm again after he learned to channel his inner diva, Dylan and Mavis Staples did have a musical reunion in 2002 to record his gospel number "Gonna Change My Way of Thinking." Compared with the 1979 version, he sounds less like a white Negro than a soul survivor. When he rasps about sitting at the "welcome table," he sounds like he's earned the right to sing the blues. Dylan and Staples's intonation and phrasing wouldn't have sounded so uncannily alike back when she was rebuffing his marriage proposal. This is the millennial Dylan who shouts out to Alicia Keys on his August 2006 album, *Modern Times*. The album's title alludes to Chaplin and possibly Sartre, but it also contained a shout-out to an R&B diva born in 1980, the year of Dylan's *Saved*. "Dylan Searches for a New Soul Mate," blared a headline from the *Guardian*, offering as evidence the following lines from "Thunder on the Mountain," the album's opening track:

I was thinking about Alicia Keys, couldn't help from crying
When she was born in Hell's Kitchen, I was living down the line
I'm wondering where in the world Alicia Keys could be

The song paid homage to Memphis Minnie's 1940 "Ma Rainey," but it outlined an obsession that was all his own. Dylan seems curious about Keys in part because he has made himself more like her— an affinity not lost on Todd Haynes when he considered casting Beyoncé as one of the six actors playing Dylan in *I'm Not There*. Dylan's earlier lyrics alluded to his interracial eroticism, but his more recent work shows how much he has come to embody his former muses.

The older Dylan became, the more he lost the upper part of his vocal range, and the more he would lean on blues inflections. Age would make him the grizzled blues man he had aspired to be when he was belting out Bukka White covers in those early busking days on Bleecker Street. Dylan told many tall tales to Nat Hentoff in the liner notes to *Freewheelin' Bob Dylan*, but he was sincere when he said, "I don't carry myself yet the way that Big Joe Williams, Woody Guthrie, Leadbelly and Lightnin' Hopkins have carried themselves. I hope to be able to someday, but they're older people." As the years went on, he would acknowledge his subjectivity while simultaneously gaining authority. "Every time you hear an expansive white man drop into his version of black English, you are witnessing minstrelsy's unconscious return," wrote Eric Lott in a blackface minstrelsy book that eventually inspired Dylan's album title (Lott, 5). In Dylan's case, the return was as conscious as possible, and he has made his audience more conscious of it as well; by the time he used the title, he had become one with the "charcoal gypsy maidens" strutting their feathers. After he saturated his 2002 film *Masked and Anonymous* with minstrel sounds and images (including a blacked-up Ed Harris, who asks Dylan's character Jack Fate, "Do you remember me?"), he brought the mask of minstrelsy up to the surface, haunted by its history, fascinated by its legacy. In the film, Dylan actually performs two minstrel songs—"Diamond Joe" and "Dixie"— and then has an exchange with Oscar Vogel (Ed Harris), while an actual black man with dreadlocks hovers over him, a repetition of Dylan's mystical racial transference. "Do you remember?" asks Vogel. Jack Fate is not so sure, but Dylan himself has become explicitly aware of how he has borrowed and appropriated, loved and thieved. Now that he has reinvented himself as rock's elder statesman of letters, he can look back on his midlife crisis as a time when he was still earning the right to sing the blues, looking to the Queens of Rhythm to help him preach. Back in 1964, he sang "The night is pitch black, come an' make my / Pale face fit into place, ah, please!" But what had once been a sign of selling out became a source of his salvation. He has now become his own cultural studies theorist and his own black backup singer. Few American figures could have crossed such racial terrain and emerged with a cultural studies thesis of their own. It was Dylan's tendency to disappear in his personae that made it easier to abandon the Queens of Rhythm when he moved on. Blackness has been a trope that just won't quit. He will likely continue to find new ways of engaging with it—with his phrasing, his blues, his eccentric sense of swing and soul—for the rest of his career.

"I've been wading through the high muddy waters," Dylan sang on "Tryin' to Get to Heaven" in 1997. By then, he sounded like he had finally arrived; on the way, he shared a stage with Waters himself. The year was 1975, a decade after "Like a Rolling Stone" railed against Miss Lonely and her Waters pretensions. At New York's Bottom Line, invited to play harmonica at a Waters show, Dylan was up on stage with the real thing. Flanked by the near-suicide Phil Ochs on one side and blues diva Victoria Spivey on the other, he was still cultivating the ad hoc club atmosphere that would become the Rolling Thunder Revue. Waters knew someone important was backstage, pimping out the entourage and generating the buzz, but he didn't know who it was. He announced to the audience, "We have a special guest on harmonica. Please give a nice round of ac-clause (that's how Muddy pronounced applause and no one ever corrected him) for . . . JOHN DYLAN." A few people clapped politely until guitarist Bob Margolin stage-whispered in Waters's ear, "His name is Bob, like my name—Bob Dylan." Waters then repeated, "Bob Dylan!" as if he had said it for the first time, inspiring pande-monium. Whether Waters was pulling a fast one on Dylan or not, Dylan probably wanted to get as far away from himself as he could at that moment. He was face to face with his metaphor, and his metaphor claimed not to know who he was. But Dylan knew full well who Waters was, and was happy just to blow his harp in the background, trying to summon his inner rolling stone while he watched the man himself at work. After nearly half a century of imi-tating, protesting, loving, and thieving, he is still trying to earn the right to sing the blues. A lyric about mortality from 1997 could also apply to his transformation: He's not dark yet, but he's getting there.

"Even the President of the United States . . ."

Until 2008, Dylan had never endorsed a presidential candidate.

Even Jimmy Carter, who invited him as a White House guest, and Bill Clinton, who summoned him to sing at his inaugural and presented him with a Kennedy Center Award (they joined hands, flanked by other recipients, singing "God Bless America"), did not get a thumbs-up. All this changed when, in an interview with the *London Times* in June of the election year, Dylan finally jumped into the presidential fray: "We've got this guy out there now who is redefining the nature of politics from the ground up . . . Barack Obama. He's redefining what a politician is, so we'll have to see how things play out. Am I hopeful? Yes, I'm hopeful that things might change. Some things are going to have to" ("Dylan Says Barack Obama Is 'Changin' America," Alan Jackson and David Byers, *Times Online*, June 5, 2008).

Dylan went on to speak ebulliently about Obama's first memoir, *Dreams from My Father*: "He's like a fictional character, but he's real," Dylan would say later, the highest compliment imaginable from this source.[5] He might have recognized a fellow shape-shifter. He did not make reference to the idea of the first black president; he perhaps felt it was unnecessary. Obama, in turn, said he had "Maggie's Farm" along with other Dylan songs on his iPod, and that it summed up his feelings about the campaign trail. "Someone asked me if I'm registered to vote," sings a jaded Dylan on "Highlands." Nevertheless, it was probably no accident that Dylan, for election day, scheduled a performance in Northrop Auditorium, Minneapolis, a town where he not only owns property but might even be registered to vote. When he opened with "Cat's in the Well," it was anyone's election. (No one knew if they could believe the polls.) When it was over, the confetti had started flying. Dylan made an extremely rare public statement, after going through the usual motions of introducing the band: "I wanna introduce my band right now. . . . Tony Garnier, wearin' the Obama button—[applause] alright!—Tony likes to think it's a brand new time right now. An age of light. Me, I was born in 1941—that's the year they bombed Pearl Harbor. Well, I been livin' in a world of darkness ever since. But it looks like things are gonna change now . . . ." What followed was a "Blowin' in the Wind" like none other, gypsy-flavored and never more apropos. "Yes, 'n' how many years can some people exist / Before they're allowed to be free?" Dylan sang, knowing that this question finally had an answer. Obama was not yet two years old when that record was first released. His blackness was self-taught. Dylan was witnessing a new kind of New Frontier. Obama would face hysterical opposition the minute he set foot in 1600 Pennsylvania Avenue, but his right to be free was no longer the question (even if his birth certificate was). Things had indeed changed, but it was too soon to know what they were changing into.

For Black History Month in February 2010, President Obama scheduled a concert saluting the music of the civil rights movement. A blizzard sidelined many of the scheduled performers. The only white ones, Dylan and Joan Baez, were also the only artists on the bill who had actually sung at the March on Washington. Despite rumors, their performances were separate. Dylan was prepared to do a three-song set that included "Blowin' in the Wind" and "Chimes of Freedom," but when it turned out that only one was called for, perhaps he thought about that interview and went for "The Times, They Are a-Changin'." The times, they had. Obama was entering his second year in the White House and would eventually, on a party line vote, succeed in passing sweeping healthcare reform. He must have taken satisfaction at hearing lines that applied to civil rights, which would also apply to his own embattled agenda:

Come senators, congressmen
Please heed the call
Don't stand in the doorway
Don't block up the hall

Obama thanked Dylan for "taking time off from his never-ending tour," but in fact he was off the road at the time, planning an Asian tour for the spring (where he would still be subversive enough to be kicked out of China). Dylan had kept his guitar playing at a minimum since 2003, and the sight of him holding an acoustic guitar was particularly rare, but he must have been aware of the symbolism—a machine that, like Woody's, kills fascists. With pianist Patrick Warren filling in the chords, and longtime bassist (the one wearing the Obama button on election night) Tony Garnier on upright, Dylan strummed just a little (in a precise arrangement) and picked not at all. His vocals were strained on the high notes but impassioned and lucid. There was no sneering, no irony, and no incoherence. He was locked into the waltz, announcing change for the millionth time. A seismic one had actually happened, and was continuing to happen. History was moving forward, blackness would have a new symbolic meaning, and he was somehow a part of it. There is a photo of the two men. Obama is seated with the first lady, relaxed, smiling. Dylan is standing, shaking Obama's hand. His face is the personification of glee. He is beaming, with an open-mouthed smile, full of light. It is not Dylan's usual expression, but this was no usual moment. That night, his decades-long engagement with black culture was reaching a closed circle. Decades earlier, he provided music for freedom riders. Later he had made his debut at the Apollo and had given his first presidential endorsement to Obama. Now he was being endorsed back. The whole wide world, as he sang at Martin Luther King's podium in 1963, was watchin'. It would be watchin' yet again. The world of darkness Dylan was born into now had a crack of light. Anything could happen.

FOUR

Don't Steal, Don't Lift

Appropriation, Artifice, Originality

"Must I Always Be the Thief?"

"Bob is not authentic at all. He's a plagiarist, and his name and voice are fake. Everything about Bob is a deception. We are like night and day, he and I." These words were spoken by Joni Mitchell in 2010, and, after they were published in the *Los Angeles Times*, they invoked impassioned defenses that reverberated throughout the blogosphere, an entity that Dylan couldn't have fathomed when he stole his first batch of 78s. The most prominent apologia was by the estimable historian Sean Wilentz, who, writing in *The Daily Beast*, defended Dylan on the grounds that everything the man filches he transfigures: "This isn't just a matter of law or ethics. It's a matter of the illusions we make in order to live, which is one definition of art. Dylan, an artist, steals what he loves and then loves what he steals by making it new." Here we get a mix of love, theft, and Ezra Pound, whose mantra of newness remains forever young. But are all thefts alike? Is Mitchell, a member of an extremely small peer group of singer-songwriters with Dylan, Leonard Cohen, and a few others, missing subtlety and allusion, while his fiercest partisans will defend the most flagrant appropriations? Dylan began his career stealing from Woody Guthrie, but with affection and a nod to the source. He then became so inspired, stray lines from here or there became part of the alchemy. But what about when he was less inspired? How much can you lean on your source material until it is no longer yours? Dylan doesn't deserve Mitchell's denouncement. But the lines between allusion and appropriation have nevertheless taken on new proportions in the case of Dylan in the twenty-first century. The millennial Dylan is not entirely a deception, but he doesn't always come clean, either.

"Look Out, Kid"

The monochrome footage accompanying "Subterranean Homesick Blues," used as the opening of D. A. Pennebaker's *Dont Look Back*, shows an indelible image of Dylan, including advice he was not inclined to follow. It was shot in the beginning of 1965, a year that would become a fetish object in the world of Dylanography. Dylan, an immodest twenty-three, stands in the alley of London's Savoy Hotel, holding signs scrawled with selected words from the song. With his baby face, James Dean sneer, and frizzy pompadour, he affects a calculated insouciance. While we hear the song playing, he is not lip-syncing but tossing aside placards one at a time, stone faced. He wants us to focus on the words—bad puns, clichés, and random maxims—but he also wants to give the impression that he couldn't care less about them. The recording spews out the associative lyrics faster than Dylan can toss aside "LOOK OUT" and "KID." By the time he gets to the end of each verse, he is throwing the placards faster and faster. It's the music driving the words, not the other way around.

This is one of the most ubiquitous images in rock and roll, created a decade and a half before the launch of MTV, alluded to in videos by INXS, the Red Hot Chili Peppers, even a parody in the YouTube Democratic presidential debate in the summer of 2007. This was a hard image to resist, a rock and roll that could read. The rock-and-roll attitude was certainly about indifference, although it was accompanied by convoluted word play. The words went by fast, but a lot of it rang true enough for Bartlett's: "The pump don't work, 'cause the vandals took the handle," "Twenty years of schooling and they put you on the day shift." Others had more direct impact. "You don't need a weatherman to know which way the wind blows" was ominously co-opted by the radical group the Weatherman, which included three members who would accidentally die in an explosion in Manhattan's Greenwich Village, ignoring the advice he gives elsewhere in the song: "Don't follow leaders." In Pennebaker's iconic footage, Dylan, almost contemptuously, lets the placards reading "WIND BLOWS" fall aside like garbage.

Allen Ginsberg, who scrawled some of the words himself, hovers near a garbage can, dovening like an Orthodox rabbi, supporting the premise that Dylan took the aesthetic of *Howl* and set it to a rockabilly riff; he was an Elvis and a Kerouac in a Jewish punk with no shortage of attitude, who looks like he's too young to shave. (Whether or not it mattered that Dylan's favorite living poet was consigned to a trash can was another matter.) This was the Dylan who inspired Bruce Springsteen to say at Dylan's 1988 induction to the Rock and Roll Hall of Fame, "The way Elvis freed your body, Dylan freed your mind." This was the young man who crowds still somehow want to see, even though he is as inaccessible as the era he has come to embody. "Subterranean Homesick Blues" combined derivative sources for an effect that was startlingly original. The song's lyrics had some striking similarities to Woody Guthrie and Pete Seeger's "Taking It Easy," its riff sounded appropriated from

Chuck Berry's "Too Much Monkey Business," and its title was a nod to Jack Kerouac. He was not claiming purity in his findings— random utterances and recycled wisdom, and, in the Pennebaker footage, not even all scrawled in his own hand—even though he did claim a composer's credit. Did this vandal take the handle? And was that really the whole point? Dylan is heard singing "Don't steal, don't lift," while is he seen lifting a placard reading "DON'T LIFT." A year earlier, when Dylan was on the *Steve Allen Show*, he was asked, "Do you sing your own songs or other people's?" The cryptic response was pure Dylan: "They're all mine, now." He *was* being sincere in that he had made the move from folk artist to original singer-songwriter, but he was also not far from the era where melodies were passed around like so many hats rattling for cover charge, when a melody taught to Dylan by Paul Clayton could emerge as the breakup masterpiece "Don't Think Twice, It's Alright."

"Don't steal, don't lift." The lines resonate over four decades later, but with a new irony. Dylan, who David Hajdu called the "Elvis of the mind," has been accused of stealing and lifting material used in a growing chunk of his twenty-first-century output. Building on the models of Woody Guthrie, Chuck Berry, and Little Richard, Dylan transformed the entire idea of a singer-songwriter and combined pop songwriting with dense poetic influence. He was a rock-and-roll Rimbaud, a plugged-in Beat. But recently he has been revealed to be leaning more and more on his source material, some well known, some obscure. Sometimes he alludes, but other times he plunders and buries. "It's easy to see without looking too far that not much is really sacred," he sang in 1965. Four decades and later, what seemed like prophecy became fate: Dylan himself has since become sacred to many, and it was disturbing to find that if you examined his recent work, you found a committee of muses. Marcel Proust, Jack London, and Mark Twain were among those lifted in his beguiling, best-selling, effusively reviewed, and National Book Award–nominated

memoir *Chronicles, Vol. I*.[1] After the associative incoherence of his novel *Tarantula* (1971)—a sophomoric Joyce imitation that without a rock star byline would have languished on a publisher's slush pile—reviewers were shocked by the clarity, the lucidity, the humor, the plain-spoken self-deprecation of his autobiographical writing. Then it turned out that, at least in some sections, he was still writing cut-and-paste prose: he just made it look seamless. Yet Dylan has always stolen, making optimal use of whatever he found—all the way back to when he stole some of his first blues records on the way to his 1961 trip to New York City in the name of being a "musical expeditionary." It is of no small significance that *Chronicles* begins and ends in the office of music publisher Lou Levy; what began as folk art was becoming something that would generate royalties; he was becoming something of his own invention. In the folk clubs, they passed renditions for gigs the way they passed the hat for small amounts of cash. Once Dylan was seated in Levy's office, he was becoming something else, something that, on the level of royalties and many others, was becoming his own invention. There is much that Dylan leaves out of *Chronicles*, but he bookends it with Levy, and this emphasis is deliberate. Music publishing would distinguish him from the old Gerdes' Folk City Crowd.

"I look upon fine Phrases like a Lover," wrote Keats;[2] Dylan looked upon Proust's fine phrases (in Scott Moncrieff's translation) like an abductor. "Plagiarism" literally means "abduction"—itself hijacked from the ancient Greek "plagion"—and it is a fine line between picking up those placards and actually stealing and lifting. The passage in *Chronicles* where Dylan steals and lifts Proust is a description of a moment when, ironically, Dylan questions whether he should go on as a writer. It is 1987, and he is at a career low point, in the midst of recording two of the least-loved albums in his catalogue: *Knocked Out Loaded* (1986), whose sole redeeming track is the majestic "Brownsville Girl," co-written with the playwright and actor Sam Shepard, and *Down in the Groove* (1988), whose strongest song, "Silvio," was co-written with Grateful Dead lyricist Robert Hunter. At this point in the book, Dylan contemplates his musical future while recovering from a hand injury, even considering half-baked business schemes, until he began writing the songs for *Oh Mercy* (1989), a comeback album that is given a track-by-track description in the book. The songs, he wrote, "came from out of the blue" (165). But before he begins his exegesis of the album, he describes a moment of contemplation as he walks to his house: "Walking back to the main house, I caught a glimpse of the sea through the leafy boughs of the pines. I wasn't near it, but could feel the power beneath its colors" (162).

Anyone writing a memoir might feel the pressure to make it Proustian. Dylan apparently addressed this by actually culling Proust. The quoted sentences were cobbled together from a paragraph from Proust's *Within a Budding Grove*. It is a moment when Proust's Marcel (his eponymous narrator) describes gaining a perspective on perspective: "But when, Mme. de Villeparisis's carriage having reached high ground, *I caught a glimpse of the sea through the leafy boughs of trees*, then no doubt at such a distance those temporal details which had set the sea, as it were, apart from nature and history disappeared. . . . But on the other hand *I was no longer near enough to the sea which seemed to me not a living thing now, but fixed; I no longer felt any power beneath its colours*, spread like those of a picture among the leaves, through which it appeared as inconsistent as the sky and only of an intenser blue" (536–37, italics added). His description uses Proust's language to convey the opposite experience. In the previous sections of *In Search of Lost Time*, "Place Names: The Name" and "Place Names: The Place," Proust describes the enchantment of names and the disenchantment of visiting the places they describe that never match one's imaginings of them. Proust describes Marcel seeing a sea, as if through a frame, but he can no longer feel the sea's power beneath its colors. In this passage, Dylan claims that he *does* feel the power of the sea's colors, and he will soon go on to regain his songwriting powers, although now we have learned more about his process of inspiration. While Dylan is describing feeling uninspired before being moved to create, he slips into some phrases of Proust, as if speaking in tongues.

Writing a book certainly wasn't as easy as songwriting for Dylan. "While you're writing, you're not living," he told David Gates in 2004 in a *Newsweek* cover story promoting the book. "What do they call it? Splendid isolation? I don't find it that splendid." In that less than splendid isolation, Dylan did what he often does when pressed for material: he reached into his box. Dylan has said that he stores up material in a box—containing snippets from books, movies, and probably conversation—that he dips into when he needs inspiration. Many of the lines from *Empire Burlesque* (1985), for example, came from *The Maltese Falcon* and other noir films. "I didn't write that," he would claim about a particular song. "The box is writing the song." By the time Dylan recorded *Modern Times* (2006), the box had become quite busy indeed.[3]

Dylan began his career redefining authorship for pop music. *Bob Dylan* (1961), Dylan's first album, which initially sold around 2,500 copies and got him labeled as "Hammond's folly," contained only two originals, both of them overtly, even deferentially, indebted to "Woody, Cisco, and Leadbelly, too." "Hey, hey, Woody Guthrie, I wrote you a song," he sang on that album's "Song to Woody," a brash statement from a nineteen-year-old upstart, albeit one who was still a blushing acolyte, shamelessly using the melody of Guthrie's "1913 Massacre." It was not until *Freewheelin' Bob Dylan* (1963) that Hammond's folly became, as Robert Shelton predicted in his 1961 *New York Times* review, "the brilliant singing poet laureate of young America." If he hadn't made the move from the traditional "Highway 51" to the original "Highway 61 Revisited" of 1965, he would not be a "poet laureate" but just among dime-a-dozen Guthrie imitators on MacDougal Street, some of whom had better guitar chops and more precise vocal skills. When Dylan emerged as a songwriter on his second album, he was shifting agency from the tunesmith to the performer, ushering an *auteur*-theory era of pop music. His songs, unlike those of Elvis, Bing, or Sinatra, were not cooked up by Tin Pan Alley tunesmiths but were all emanating from the young man with the Huck Finn cap. (And to the delight of his Svengali manager Albert Grossman, all royalties went to him, too.) He may have hated the tag "voice of a generation," but being a mere imitator would have been unbearable.

Nearly half a century later, as his status continues to rise in the literary and academic world, his box is returning songwriting back to the anonymous and communal. Something called "the folk process" is usually offered in Dylan's line of defense, defined by Charles Seeger, a Harvard musicologist and father of Pete, as "by definition, and, as far as we can tell, by reality, entirely a product of plagiarism." But the folk process created folk songs. Dylan ceased to be a folk artist in 1963, and he was accused of plagiarism then, too, when a high school student named Lorre Wyatt claimed that Dylan had "stolen" the title of "Blowin' in the Wind" from him, a charge he later retracted. By 1978, Dylan at least revealed the song's source: "'Blowin' in the Wind' has always been a spiritual. I took it off a song, I don't know if you ever heard, called 'No More Auction Block.'" The chords, not the words and not really the melody, do resemble the antislavery anthem, immortalized in the chilling Odetta version that inspired the teenage Dylan to go acoustic, but "Blowin' in the Wind" is certainly independent of its origins. "Steal a little and they put you in jail / Steal a lot and they make you king," sang Dylan in "Sweetheart Like You," from 1983's *Infidels*, where he sings the song's refrain, "What's a sweetheart like you doing in a dump like this?" in full recognition that he was not the first guy to ask the question. Dylan has always stolen a little; more recently, he has stolen a lot. "If there's an original thought out there I could use it right now," Dylan sang in "Brownsville Girl." When Dylan was learning songs from fellow musicians on Bleecker Street, everything was shared. All that changed when he signed his name on the dotted line. Originality became not only a creative or philosophical matter but a legal one. Recording contracts made all the difference, and they changed all the expectations. His identity quickly changed from just another magpie to a major cultural entity: poet, prophet, conscience, all these words that he tried to demolish.

By the new millennium, when all these charges hit, Dylan seemed to be indestructible, and the legal battles in music publishing tended to be over sampling. That was the year when the Japanese novelist Junichi Saga (who still has an active copyright) had entire, seemingly random passages from his book *Confessions of a Yazuka* appear as lyrics credited to Dylan on *"Love and Theft"* (2001), and Henry Timrod, Poet Laureate of the Confederacy (a curio who died of tuberculosis in 1867 and whose copyright must have expired the night they drove old Dixie down) was similarly pilfered on *Modern Times* (2006). When the *Wall Street Journal* first reported that random sections of Saga's novel *Confessions of a Yakuza* appeared uncredited in several Dylan songs, Saga asked, "Bob Dylan is a famous country singer, yes?" Saga added that credit on future editions would be "very honorable," but he was dreaming. *Modern Times* (2006), which bumped Justin Timberlake off the top of the *Billboard* charts, giving Dylan his first number-one album in thirty years (and making him, at sixty-five, the oldest person to get there),[4] was strewn with plundering, though all of it (as far as we know) with dead copyrights. The album had a title that alluded to Charlie Chaplin and perhaps Jean-Paul Sartre, but it sounded like the opposite of making it new. Bing Crosby haunted "When the Deal Goes Down" (a rewrite of "Where the Blue of the Night," written by Crosby, Roy Turk, and Fred Ahlert) and "Beyond the Horizon" (which had a melody identical to that of Jimmy Kennedy and Hugh Williams's 1935 "Red Sails in the Sunset"). Anyone looking to the lyrics for intertextual clues could find this nod to a Crosby movie: "The Bells of St. Mary, how sweetly they chime / Beyond the horizon, I found you just in time."

Modern Times contained other derivations, too. On "The Levee's Gonna Break," Dylan pulled a Led Zeppelin, recycling a motif from a Memphis Minnie blues released just in time for the Hurricane Katrina anniversary. The third track on *Modern Times*, "Rollin' and Tumblin'," is the most blatant example where Dylan didn't merely take lines out of the box and fashion them into something else, but played a cover with a few added verses and called it an original. The riff and opening verse were identical to Muddy Waters's song of the same name. On Waters's *Chess Box*, the song is credited to one McKinley Morganfield—the name on Waters's birth certificate— which would be the equivalent of Dylan using the name Robert Zimmerman for his publishing, which he doesn't. But did Waters have any right to claim credit for it any more than Dylan? Absolutely not, although he didn't receive his first royalty check until the 1976 soundtrack of *The Last Waltz*, a bill headlined by Dylan. Tracing the origins of "Rollin' and Tumblin'" requires going back further, to musicians who *never* received royalties.

Robert Johnson, the "King of the Delta Blues," posthumously worshipped and imitated by Eric Clapton, Mick Jagger, Keith Richards, and, in various lines, Dylan, originally used the verse ("I rolled and tumbled, I cried the whole night long") on "If I Had Possession on Judgment Day," and Johnson is credited as the songwriter—not that he was alive to receive such an album credit. As stirring as his performance is, though, Johnson does not really have possession of the song any more than he does over Judgment Day. The earliest known recording of this verse and riff is from Hambone Willie

Newbern from 1929: "Roll and Tumble Blues." It is more than likely that Newbern didn't write "Rollin' and Tumblin'" either, although the recorded trail stops there. Apparently, Dylan figured he might as well join in with Muddy Waters to claim composer's credit for "Rollin' and Tumblin'," since no one really owned it anyway. It could have been a work song, even a slave song. It is now public domain, and while anyone can claim credit for it, its real origins will remain obscure. Each version of "Rollin' and Tumblin'" contains its own variations, and Dylan's includes lines like "Some young lazy slut has charmed away my brains," which contain a certain gravity only because of the aura he has created for himself. Who he is, not what he is actually singing, makes one wonder exactly what he meant. No one would be wondering if Mick Jagger had sung it.

We do wonder about what Dylan meant, though, and in a different way than we do about Waters, Johnson, or Newbern. None of them conducted such a hierarchical balancing act between highbrow and low down, exiting where Mona Lisa must have had the highway blues. "All songs written by Bob Dylan," said the credit on *Modern Times*, but "written" was becoming a relative term. Were these appropriations the sign of a waning muse, or was Dylan merely doing a version of what he has always done? Sometimes Dylan leans on the box in odd ways that still indicate genius: turning stray lines by a dead, obscure poet or living Japanese novelist into a Bob Dylan song amounts to a kind of found object art. On other instances, on *Modern Times*, he is hewing so close to his source material, he is stretching the bounds of authorship. Dylan has been attacked aggressively and defended extravagantly (more so than anyone else would be if faced with similar charges). But is extreme attack or complete inoculation beside the point? The Dylan effect has always been complicated. He has often been less than forthcoming with his sources, and he has centuries of tradition to back him up—from the "folk process" to high modernism. Was Dylan betraying his identity as a writer, or had he been making his audience—at least those able to read between the lines—rethink the concept of originality?

"These fragments I have shored against my ruins," wrote T. S. Eliot in *The Waste Land,* and Dylan has been shoring up these fragments against his own impending mortality, while perfecting a character of an older man in heartbreak. The blues he intones in a ragged croon or sometimes desperate croak sounds more authentic than it did in a younger man's snarl. Dylan has become the King Lear of rock and roll, raging against the heath, or at least the tie-dyed *hoi polloi* at his concerts. But the writing is more dependent on the words of others. His two cover albums in the 1990s got Dylan back to the career renaissance he enjoyed with what was called—to his protest—his late-career "trilogy": *Time Out of Mind, "Love and Theft,"* and *Modern Times.* In 1992 and 1993, when the inconsistency of Dylan's later work seemed like a foregone conclusion, Dylan made two albums of traditional songs just as the craze in "roots" music was a fringe phenomenon, a sliver of the cult of authenticity that dominated the folk scene that Dylan entered in 1961. Dylan had built up such loyalty among his fan base—which, it seemed, was dominating his critical base—that he could endure every plagiarism charge that came his way. "To live outside the law, you must be honest," sang Dylan in a famous line that resembled one from Don Neil's 1958 film *The Lineup.* Living outside the law would be just fine for many in Dylan's audience, a law that was hardly ironclad to begin with. Going back to the source was just what the icon needed.

"The Songs Are My Lexicon"

In 1997, Dylan emerged from the hospital for treatment for histoplasmosis, a rare, potentially fatal fungal infection of the heart. "I really thought I'd be seeing Elvis soon," he quipped. Dylan's survival would mark a turning point in his career as dramatic as his motorcycle accident from 1966, which may or may not have been the cataclysmic event it had been made out to be. He emerged from a moribund state in more ways than one: *The Bootleg Series* in 1991 confirmed what seemed obvious to those who wanted him to live up to his best work: he had, in spite of the intermittent great songs and performances, become something of an idiot-savant version of himself. Some of his best songs were ending up on the cutting room floor, and some of the worst were ending up on his commercially issued albums. What could have possessed him to leave "Blind Willie McTell" off *Infidels* or "Dignity" off *Oh Mercy*? And why was he then choosing to include "Wiggle Wiggle" on *Under the Red Sky?* There is a YouTube clip titled "The Worst Song From The Worst Concert EVER!"posted by a person with the screen name rankflv—who, in possession of hundreds of concert clips, would be in a position to know. The concert was from a European tour from the summer of 1991, the year Dylan turned fifty, when he was really testing his faithful. He is clearly drunk at this concert, slurring his words when he uncharacteristically speaks to the audience as the song is already beginning: "This is off my last record. It sold a lot and it's gonna sell a lot more." It is not known what state he was in when he wrote "Wiggle Wiggle," but one wonders what could possibly explain lines like these:

> Wiggle 'til you're high, wiggle 'til you're higher,
> Wiggle 'til you vomit fire,
> Wiggle 'til it whispers, wiggle 'til it hums,
> Wiggle 'til it answers, wiggle 'til it comes.

"Vomit fire"? This seemed like a placeholder that never got replaced.[5] How could this be the Dylan who wrote "Visions of Johanna"? It was clear Dylan needed a sabbatical from songwriting. At what must have been a truly low point, he collaborated with Michael Bolton on the song "Steel Bars" for Bolton's multi-platinum *Time, Love, and Tenderness.*

Baby boomer rock icons were finding middle age awkward as the 1980s lumbered on. When Dylan was asked at his notoriously belligerent 1965 San Francisco press conference to define himself for those over thirty, Dylan, at twenty-five, proudly defined himself as under thirty. Now he was fifty and didn't seem to know how to consistently exploit it for artistic gain. Synthesizers and echo-chamber drums sounded like desperation, the sonic equivalent of scratchy polyester under fluorescent light, particularly anachronistic with a middle-aged voice of an earlier, analog generation. It was a sound that was particularly problematic for Dylan, who, while sonically obsessed, was also conspicuously passive about it, even on some of his masterpieces. Mighty classics like *Highway 61 Revisited* and *Blood on the Tracks* were often woefully out of tune—perhaps out of indifference, perhaps in the tradition of the folk classics he revered, made with resources considerably more limited than those of Columbia's Studio A. (The out-of-tune saloon piano in "Just Like Tom Thumb's Blues" is surely a deliberate example.) In a celebrated quotation from an interview with Ron Rosenbaum (one that even became the title of a bootleg CD), the "thin wild mercury sound" of *Blonde on Blonde* happened by a chance encounter between members of the Hawks (the proto-Band) and Nashville session musicians who had no idea who the man with the rambling, drug-induced verses even was. But while performances with seasoned Nashville musicians created just the right musical *frisson* in 1966, working with synthesizers on *Empire Burlesque* in 1985 (Dylan can be seen on the cover looking like he could be playing a drug dealer on *Miami Vice*) made it sound like he was living in someone else's moment, and some underrated songs (like "I'll Remember You," which resurfaced beautifully in *Masked and Anonymous* in 2003) were buried in the overproduced mix. Dylan made one of his periodic comebacks in

1989 with *Oh Mercy*, an album that gets a song-by-song recollection in *Chronicles, Vol. 1*. Producer Daniel Lanois helped him use age as an atmospheric effect, and even if Dylan could not respond to Lanois's request to write songs like "Masters of War," he did give him songs like the moving "Shooting Star" (a haunting elegy addressed to someone who died tragically, perhaps The Band's keyboardist Richard Manuel, who committed suicide in 1987), and the simple, finely wrought "Where Teardrops Fall." Dylan's scratchy voice was part of the set design of a swampy journey into heartbreak and regret. "She gone with the man with the long black coat," Dylan rasped, sounding like someone who had lived in the song. His voice, at forty-seven, actually sounded much older than it was. This wasn't the sound of waning fecundity. This was *gravitas*. Baby boomers could hear the swami of their generation sounding like he was intoning from the mountain, or maybe a beatific Delta swamp. Then he followed it up with *Under the Red Sky* (1990), the album that contained "Wiggle Wiggle," and the effect seemed like a mirage, another comeback derailed, Dylan demystified yet again. In retrospect, the album sounds like the precursor to an incipient resurgence, and the album's nursery rhyme–inspired lyrics have their charms, including a title track, which sounds like Dr. Seuss meets Gertrude Stein (a little girl and a little boy, by the light of the man in the moon, get baked in a pie) and has a perfect guitar solo from George Harrison (and, in a bizarre pop culture collision, Randy Jackson, later of *American Idol*, on bass).

Still, in 1991, in spite of some brilliant performances here and there, Dylan appeared to be crumbling in public, although his badness was fascinating in its way. A peak of this period that was widely seen showed how gleefully he seemed to be defacing his own icon; the self-defacement is, in fact, a crucial *part* of his iconography. On February 20, 1991, he accepted a Lifetime Achievement Grammy, and even though the event was pronounced evidence of his incoherence, in retrospect it can also be seen as a precursor to his icon restoration. He later claimed to be suffering from a cold that day, and his presentation was somehow willfully phlegmatic. The ceremony happened to be held during the three days of combat of the first Gulf War. Dylan had abandoned politics, for the most part, since late 1963, when he drunkenly told the crowd at the American Civil Liberties Union that he identified with Lee Harvey Oswald. But for some reason, he used this award as a moment to make a political statement with a blistering version of his 1963 jeremiad "Masters of War," a song that makes up for its lack of subtlety with a devastating visceral assault. In 1963, Dylan was writing what he called "fingerpointing" songs, but "Masters of War" was more of a hex, an invective against military-industrial complex bureaucrats who pushed papers while young soldiers—around the age of the twenty-one-year-old Dylan of the song when he wrote it—were sent off to combat. Dylan later admitted that he had teenage ambitions to enter West Point and even romanticized the idea of dying heroically in battle; he finally made it to West Point in 1990 to perform "Masters of War." Although it wasn't mentioned in the songwriting credit, the song's melody was based on the traditional "Nottamun Town," for which the Scottish singer Jean Ritchie tried and failed to claim credit in an unsuccessful lawsuit the year after the song was released on *Freewheelin' Bob Dylan*. But Dylan was not providing any 1960s time warp that night at the Grammy Awards. It was very much the year of Operation Desert Storm, and Dylan, in adenoidal despair, snarled out the song in a nearly unintelligible jumble while his band thrashed behind him. The song's final unforgiving lines seemed inspired by William Wyler's 1941 film *The Little Foxes*, in which Betty Davis likewise exclaims, "And I hope that you die, and your death will come soon!" On the 1991 version, it was a death wish few could understand, drowned out by feedback and gargling phlegm. Dylan never spoke publicly about his views on the American invasion of

Vietnam or, later, Iraq, but he did give this odd piece of performance art during an apropos moment.

When the time came to accept the award, presented with cinematic verve by Jack Nicholson, Dylan stumbled on stage and nearly walked off without saying a word. But he knew he had to say something, and he seemed in the spirit of the song's relentless bile, where gratitude of any kind would seem disingenuous. Wearing a porkpie hat indoors, shifting his feet, and looking for as quick an escape as possible, he broke into an impression of a Steinbeck character, sounding like he was emanating from the Dust Bowl by way of absolutely nowhere: "Well, my daddy, he didn't leave me much, you know he was a very simple man, but what he did tell me was this [long pause followed by uncomfortable laughter, reveling in the possibility that on live television, anything is possible]. He said so many things, you know. He did say, son, he said 'you know it's possible to become so defiled in this world that your own father and mother will abandon you and if that happens, God will always believe in your ability to mend your ways.'" Dylan makes his "daddy" sound more like an Okie farmer than a secretary-treasurer of an appliance store, but the source of the statement was definitely from the world of his fathers, bearing a striking resemblance to Psalms 27:10: "When my father and my mother forsake me, then the LORD will take me up," but an even closer resemblance was to nineteenth-century German rabbi Shimshon Rafael Hirsch: "Even if I were so depraved that my own mother and father would abandon me to my own devices, God would still gather me up and believe in my ability to mend my way." This was the period when Dylan appeared on Chabad telethons, playing harmonica on "Hava Negilah" (accompanied by Harry Dean Stanton), shilling the television audience for donations. Dylan may or may not have been invoking actual advice from Abraham Zimmerman. The answer was blowing in something: a Hasidic prayer book, a Scottish ballad, his own back pages.

There would be more awards to accept, more wars to protest, and the old words would keep coming in handy. And, for a while, there was nowhere to go but public domain.

On October 16, 1992, Dylan gave a glitzy salute to his past at a Madison Square Garden concert celebrating his thirty years as a recording artist, and while there were notable heartfelt versions of his songs from Neil Young, George Harrison, and others, it was most memorable for Sinead O'Connor getting booed offstage, shortly after her career-destroying appearance on *Saturday Night Live* a week earlier when she ripped up a picture of the Pope. The mob who hooted O'Connor off stage were there to cheer on Dylan, who performed uncertain versions of his old standards, still trying to hit the notes he had belted out decades earlier, not sure about what his next incarnation would be. While he was certainly giving stronger performances on more inspired nights in lower profile settings, clues to his next incarnation would appear in two traditional folk albums that would appear: *Good as I Been to You* (1992) and *World Gone Wrong* (1993). With his out-of-tune guitar and low-fi equipment— the albums were casually and quickly recorded in Dylan's garage—it was all too easy to dismiss them as mere obligations, fulfilling the end of a Columbia contract that would eventually be renewed. But Dylan sounds liberated singing the words of others, freed from the albatross of past expectations, from studio technology and from any sonic indication that he is living in the moment of, as he puts it in the *World Gone Wrong* liner notes, "celestial grunge." Celestial finger-picking, Carter Family–style, was preferable for Dylan, sitting out the zeitgeist in his Malibu garage.

Shortly after recording *Good as I Been to You*, Dylan said of the traditional material, "I treated them as if they were my songs, not like covers," and on both albums, his personality is stamped on every track: just as he told Steve Allen in 1964, they're all his, now. Some reviewers complained about the loss of range and dexterity in

Dylan's voice, but they were missing the point. Dylan exploited every crack and crevice in an instrument long weathered by decades of smoking. But what he lost in dexterity, he more than made up for in drama. Its wreckage, in fact, was crucial for the delivery. The title track of *World Gone Wrong*, slightly but crucially altered from the Mississippi Sheiks' "The World Is Going Wrong," is an example of how an aging rock star could summon a different kind of *weltzschmerz* than black Depression-era troubadours who would go back to sharecropping a few years after recording the song. The chorus's refrain uses apocalypse as a convenient excuse for bad behavior: "I can't be good no more, just like I done before / I can't be good, baby, honey because the world's gone wrong." The Mississippi Sheiks play this for comedy, as if to show that, even in the face of depression, a scoundrel is still a scoundrel. Dylan, a few keys lower and a little slower, makes it sadder, more resigned, intractable. The world is not, in the words of the Sheiks' original title, *going* wrong. It has already gone wrong, with no turning back. Dylan, with his hat and cane, greets the world's wrong turn with an antiquarian shrug. For "Blood in My Eyes," the other Mississippi Sheiks cover on the album (he recorded their biggest hit, "Tomorrow Night," on *Good as I Been to You*), Dylan made a video in which he wanders around London's Camden market in a jaded haze of fame, semiconsciously signing autographs, taking refuge in a café (the locale of the album's cover), where his intoning of the song's refrain, "Hey, hey baby, I've got blood in my eyes for you" is less about a young man's all-night binge than an older man's waning powers. It is not so much a serenading lover as it is a last will and testament. The Mississippi Sheiks' version is a young man's hyperbole; Dylan's anguished, strained delivery sounds almost literal. The Mississippi Sheiks broke up after 1935, and singer Bo Carter died destitute in 1964, while Dylan was on his unstoppable ascent. "There was nothing effete about The Mississippi Sheiks," Dylan wrote in the liner notes to *World Gone Wrong*, and, indeed, they are trying to sound as defiant as possible, providing buoyant entertainment in lean times.

For Dylan, though, the folk songs are like purgation, a musical mea culpa, a return to the land where it all began. "Lord, I'm broke and hungry, ragged and dirty, too," he sings on Willie Brown's "Ragged and Dirty," and he sounds convincing—at least for the latter claim. He looked to traditional songs as a ritual cleansing, with nothing but a murkily recorded acoustic guitar to back him up. Working without lyric sheets, it was as if he was summoning up Bleecker Street circa 1961, where he could have been performing the songs on a street corner, or the West 4th Street subway station. When you ain't got nothing, you've got nothing to lose, he sang in 1965, and he sounded like he was just about there, singing American songs that stretched back to the nineteenth century, and English, Scottish, and Irish ballads that stretched back centuries further. The songs told tales of adultery, plundering, murder, and deceit—of a gypsy running off with a maiden, of Stagolee, willing to shoot a man for a Stetson hat, of women who quit men for no good reason, and of men who will kill for jealousy. It was a lawless past, certainly one without copyrights or credits—yet it had a code to which Dylan pledged allegiance, and he sang and played these songs as if his life depended on it. "You're gonna quit me, baby, good as I been to you?" sang Blind Blake, not as a guilt trip, just a settling of the romantic score. *Good as I Been to You*, Dylan's 1992 album title, reminded his listeners not to give up on him just yet, even if he wasn't using his own words to make the case. The world would continue to go wrong, but Dylan the songwriter would return. But, as he would write, you can always come back, but you can't come back all the way.

"I'm just going down the road feeling bad," Dylan sang on *Time Out of Mind*, and, from the sound of his voice, you were inclined to believe him, even though "Going Down the Road Feeling Bad" was a traditional hillbilly standard warbled by Elizabeth Cotten and

Woody Guthrie back when the Dust Bowl was aswirl; it was later covered by the Grateful Dead and, in an unreleased track, Dylan and The Band from the *Basement Tapes* sessions. The line occurs when Dylan is singing about a bottomless abyss on "Tryin' to Get to Heaven": "Just when you think you've lost everything, you find out you can always lose a little more." Dylan belts the line out, exploiting his croak for all its wear and tear, emphasizing "lose" and "more" with an almost comical elongated percussive attack. How low can you go? Even more low down are the realms of Okie migration. The earliest known recording of "Going Down the Road Feeling Bad" is by Henry Whitter from 1923, and the song certainly provided the soundtrack to some harsh travels, far more arduous than that of rock and roll's most illustrious tour bus. Dylan sings the line like he is fighting for his life, and, indeed, the sessions were recorded shortly before he almost went to meet Elvis. Archaic language was wafted in elsewhere on *Time Out of Mind*'s atmospheric swamp. "I'll eat when I'm hungry, drink when I'm dry," Dylan grunted on "Standing in the Doorway," a maxim laid out on "Rye Whiskey," recorded by Woody Guthrie, and "Jack of Diamonds," recorded by Blind Lemon Jefferson back in 1926. "My heart's in the highlands, gentle and fair," he sang on the seventeen-minute closing track "Highlands," doffing his cowboy hat to a 1789 Robert Burns lyric. Yet these lines were allusive, not plagiaristic, and they were yoked together to paint a portrait of a man out of time—hence the album's title, riffing on a line uttered by Shakespeare's Mercutio in *Romeo and Juliet*. Dylan, long lauded for his originality in his strongest work, has also flirted with the boundaries between allusion and plagiarism—when a work, filled with fragments, can stand autonomously, or when the levee finally breaks. Sometimes, it is fascinating just to hear him work the archives. Back in 1970, David Bowie sang about "a strange young man called Dylan / With a voice like sand and glue." Dylan was now a strange older man, and the sand and glue were mixed with deepening regret and despair, and maybe even something like maturity. Dylan, older than that now, did something Bowie, for all his fabulous, glimmering surfaces, could never achieve: he showed us how to age in public. Rock stars were supposed to burn out, not fade away. But Dylan was growing into the character he was playing with stoicism and grace, reaching back through centuries for what was becoming the grandest late-period self-elegy in rock and roll.

"Those old songs are my lexicon and my prayer book," Dylan said in 1997 when the album was released. "All my beliefs come out of those old songs, literally, anything from 'Let Me Rest on That Peaceful Mountain' to 'Keep on the Sunny Side.' You can find all my philosophy in those old songs. I believe in a God of time and space, but if people ask me about that, my impulse is to point them back toward those songs. I believe in Hank Williams singing 'I Saw the Light.' I've seen the light, too." In 1997, *Time Out of Mind* was a new record that somehow sounded like it had always existed. Dylan had created a compelling character out of the burned-out troubadour, and even if some words and phrases were cobbled together from outside sources, whose are not? "The party's over, and there's less and less to say," Dylan conceded on "Highlands," but on a seventeen-minute track that was cut down from a staggering thirty-five minutes, Dylan still had plenty to say indeed; his archaism was his way back into the game. It came out original, as a compelling work of aural theater. "I can't even remember what it was I came here to get away from," he croons on the heart-wrenching dirge "Not Dark Yet," but even if he conveys a sublime ennui, he couldn't get away from those old songs. And to believe in a spiritual like "I Saw the Light" is to believe in a song of belief. The expression resonates beyond its subject matter; the words and sounds are intractable. If anonymous words that had resonated in the voices of Woody, Blind Lemon, or Elizabeth Cotten continued to be his lexicon, on *Time Out of Mind* he passed on the words, entangled with his own, his only lifeline to meaning.

Time Out of Mind sounded like a Sun Records session en route to deepest despair, but the belief in those old words burns out of every tortured syllable. It went triple platinum and ended up going on to win Dylan's first album of the year award. In contrast to his muddled appearance in 1991, Dylan's 1998 Grammy walk was a triumph: he won a competitive award, did not flinch when an anarchist stormed the stage with the words "Soy Bomb" emblazoned on his chest (Dylan merely arched his eyebrows when he sang "I'm love sick," continuing a devastating performance until security eventually stormed the stage), and invoked Robert Johnson and Buddy Holly in a gracious acceptance speech. The effect was continued in "Things Have Changed," his Oscar-winning song from the soundtrack of Curtis Hanson's *Wonder Boys*. It was an animus to "The Times They Are a-Changin'," and the 1963 invitation of "Come gather round people wherever you roam" gave way to the retreat of 2000: "I'm trying to get as far away from myself as I can." The Oscar still appears on stage with him at his concerts. It took seven years for "Love Sick" to appear on a Victoria's Secret commercial, but before it became a lingerie soundtrack, it was a resurrection.

"It's Rough Out There"

The apocalyptic pronouncements intoned by Dylan at least since "Hard Rain" in 1963 were eerily prescient for the September 11, 2001, release of *"Love and Theft."* It all seemed so well timed. Like "Hard Rain," a song that owed a pence or two to "Lord Randal," conceived before the Cuban Missile Crisis but forever tethered to it in the Dylanological imagination, Dylan was singing about an America headed for doom at an apropos moment. The personal intimations of mortality of *Time Out of Mind* went global. Many Dylan fans who were in New York City that day begin their 9/11 accounts with going to now-defunct Tower Records or Virgin Megastore at 9 a.m. before learning of the attacks minutes after leaving the store, clutching shopping bags containing shrink-wrapped copies of the CDs when they first viewed the burning towers. Listeners in the loop of academic cultural studies would have already known that Dylan's title was filched from Eric Lott's 1993 study of blackface minstrelsy. With his use of the title, Dylan was commenting on the counterfeit origins of rock and roll, himself included: that he was cloaking his often playful, often mournful antiquarian musings in an elaborate disguise. He had grown sick of himself and all of his creations long ago, and he had come back to tell us who we were. Life was a masquerade, and he was going to serenade us through stolen fragments and borrowed melodies, but also with love, badly needed to help the bootleg confection go down. It was an ominous tale from a cultural crypt, but told with a lot of craggy whimsy—even a knock-knock joke. Some of the riffs seemed like homages wrapped in original cloak. "Bye and Bye" 's changes were based on Leo Robin and Ralph Rainger's "Havin' Myself a Time," a song Dylan probably knew from Billie Holiday's 1938 recording, but he deserved credit for rhyming "briars" with "desires" and remarking that he still had a dream that hadn't been repossessed. Dylan's muse hadn't been repossessed, either.

In fact, he was in full possession of his powers on "Mississippi," a song amazingly left off of *Time Out of Mind*.[6] (The version on *"Love and Theft"* is more direct and unrelentingly bleak.) It is a stunning song of regret. The four syllables of "Mississippi" scanned well for the chorus, but, more crucially, it is also the land where the blues began. "Only one thing I did wrong / Stayed in Mississippi a day too long," goes the refrain. Is he confessing that he was getting too steeped in his source material? That he was wading in those twangy waters too long, no turning back? And if he waded too long, would he cross the line from love and theft to merely the latter? It's not as if he didn't warn us. "Got nothing for you, I had nothing before / Don't even have anything for myself anymore," he sings. Things should start to get interesting right about now, he promises, but in the end, mortality south of the Mason-Dixon creeps in. Before death, there is the decline of the imagination. The strains of Mississippi Delta are just too irresistible, and Dylan ripping it off is just too delicious a spectacle. We would all cross that river just to be where he is, but he's getting soaked in the Delta, wading in the waters of someone else's blues. They're all his now.

> Well, the emptiness is endless, cold as the clay
> You can always come back, but you can't come back all the way
> Only one thing I did wrong
> Stayed in Mississippi a day too long

In Mississippi, a trio of civil rights organizers in 1964—a triumvirate of two Jews and a black man—were lynched; all were presumably guided by the protest anthems of the ethnic hybrid called Dylan. It would later be the state with a senate majority leader who lost his chair but held on to his seat after he expressed nostalgia for Strom Thurmond's 1948 presidential campaign of "Segregation Forever," a state with an appallingly low per capita income and education scores. Yet it was the state of Robert Johnson, "King of the Delta Blues," according to the posthumous record that set young Robert Zimmerman chasing his ghost all the way to his 1998 Grammy speech in which he invoked Johnson's holy spirit: "The stuff we got will bust your brains out, baby," he said with all due reverence and citation. Mississippi's waters ran thick and deep, and staying in too long would be seductive, perhaps fatal. This song, written in all of Dylan's glory, his powers of expression and thoughts so sublime, was a confession to the gravitational pull of life on the Mississippi. It's lovely to be on a raft, Huck Finn said while floating down its river backwards. Dylan couldn't resist it, either. Stars and stripes, love and theft.

The waters of the Delta that tug and pull in "Mississippi" overflow in "High Water," the other standout track on *"Love and Theft."* Allusions, not plagiarisms, abound, and the words of others are entangled with his own to depict a downward cultural spiral set to a hoedown. "The cuckoo is a pretty bird / She warbles as she flies," Dylan sings on this song, and he sang the same words at the Gaslight in 1962 in a traditional English ballad also warbled by Joan Baez, Janis Joplin, the Everly Brothers, and other singers across the pond before the recording era. And when Dylan sang "I'm getting up in the morning / I believe I'll dust my broom," he was using such a famous phrase of Robert Johnson's (from the standard "Dust My Broom"), he could count on many of his listeners to be in on the riff. These lines collide with other sources not usually in the same song: George Henry Lewes (Victorian philosopher and lover of George Eliot) is arguing about cultural pluralism, Charles Darwin is trapped in Highway 5, Bertha Mason (Charlotte Brontë's madwoman in the attic) shakes and breaks an unidentified object, and Big Joe Turner is looking east and west in the dark room of his mind. Dylan snarls this in his meanest, grizzliest blues growl, and, in a song dedicated to Charley Patton, he invokes Patton's 1927 "High Water," a song as torrential as the Mississippi flood it chronicled. Patton's voice is gorgeously wrecked—apropos for a flood song—and Dylan's is pretty weatherbeaten, too. But the point of the anaphora—"High water everywhere"—is that all culture, from the blues icons, the snippets of English balladry, and scientific and humanistic modernity, is all going down in the flood. Dylan has been down this lonesome road before. "Desolation Row," the end-of-the-world finale of *Highway 61 Revisited,* also takes culture from high and low, from Ezra Pound and T. S. Eliot fighting in the captain's tower, while Ophelia, Cinderella, Einstein disguised as Robin

Hood, the Phantom of the Opera, and Casanova all join in the downward descent. Desolation Row: a carnival of culture, the last minstrel show.

There was a significant clue at the end of *"Love and Theft"* that Dylan was going to the other side of allusiveness, where the theft part of the equation takes over. On "Sugar Baby," he quips, "Some of these bootleggers / They've got pretty good stuff," and while he is among the most bootlegged artists in the history of recording, he got in on auto-bootlegging as early as the 1975 release of the 1967 *Basement Tapes*, which circulated as *The Great White Wonder*, the beginning of the fetish culture to come; his own Bootleg Series shows that he might as well profit from what others have swiped illegally. Yet the tune of "Sugar Baby" is a note-for-note dead ringer for Gene Austin's 1928 "Lonesome Road," and he even filches a line from it: "Look up look up and seek your maker fore Gabriel blows his horn." Seek the composer while you're at it. *"Love and Theft"* pilfered subtly compared with the pathological kleptomania of *Modern Times*, but it was a seductive preamble for what was ahead. Earlier on *"Love and Theft,"* on "Summer Days," Dylan riffs on *The Great Gatsby*, and, in contrast to *Confessions of a Yakuza*, he could be sure that he would have many listeners who had been through all of F. Scott Fitzgerald's books—or at least that one. Here's Dylan's version: "She says, 'You can't repeat the past.' I say, 'You can't? What do you mean, you can't? Of course you can.'" Here's an exchange between Jay Gatsby and Nick Carraway in Fitzgerald's novel: "'You can't repeat the past.' 'Can't repeat the past?' he cried incredulously. 'Why of course you can.'" Carraway is trying to talk sense into Gatsby, but he's seduced by that green light just like the rest of us. And we are seduced by the words emanating from a voice that sounds so wise and knowing, we'll take his counterfeit words. "I have my Bob Dylan mask on," Dylan said at a 1964 concert. "I'm masquerading." Gatsby was a bootlegger, one who made pretty good stuff. "They are a rotten crowd," Carraway told Gatsby. "You're worth the whole damn bunch put together!" And Dylan, we know, is worth more than the sum of his stolen parts, too. James Gatz of South Dakota, like Robert Zimmerman of Hibbing, was part artist and part con man, painting his masterpiece with an alias: "The truth was that Jay Gatsby, of West Egg, Long Island, sprang from his Platonic conception of himself. He was a son of God—a phrase which, if it means anything, means just that—and he must be about His Father's business, the service of a vast, vulgar, and meretricious beauty. So he invented just the sort of Jay Gatsby that a seventeen year old boy would be likely to invent, and to this conception he was faithful to the end."

"Try and Sit Down and Write Something Like That"

On June 10, 2007, while 12 million viewers were tuned in to "Made in America," the series finale of *The Sopranos*, 1965 Dylan surfaced on the episode's soundtrack, cutting and pasting his way into immortality. A.J. (Robert Iler) and Rhiannon (Emily Wickersham) are parked in the woods, sitting in his SUV pensively staring into space and listening intently to "It's Alright, Ma (I'm Only Bleeding)" from *Bringing It All Back Home* (1965), the album that opened with "Subterranean Homesick Blues." Earlier in the episode, at an after-funeral reception where he is surrounded by mobsters uttering banalities, A.J., who had never been a particularly introspective character until a Yeats poem (he pronounced it "Yeets") and a breakup suddenly spurred him to attempt suicide, began a rather incoherent rant about American consumerism and foreign policy. "It's like, America. . . . I mean, this is still where people come, to make it. It's a beautiful idea. And what do they get? Bling? And come ons for shit they don't need and can't afford." Later, parked in the woods and watching Rhiannon pensively smoking a cigarette and taking in the song, he hears

Dylan expressing a similar global frustration, a young man lashing out at everything around him, using a range of resources at his musical disposal. A.J. hears a man only a few years older than he is, who manages to allude to canonical literature without mispronouncing it. The hostility is focused, devastating, and, in contrast to the perception of much of Dylan's work, absolutely lucid. The Dylan of 1965 was no longer affecting the Woody Guthrie twang of a couple of years earlier, and he was not yet the adenoidal troubadour he would become in middle age. A mix of influences abound, but he's not channeling a particular dialect. The influence of the Beatles anglicized his inflections alongside the Dust Bowl and Delta blues intonations.

A.J. and Rhiannon are parked in the woods, sitting in his SUV pensively staring into space. This isn't exactly make-out music. They have been through a mental institution together and are listening for meaning. Rhiannon lights a cigarette. "Advertising signs they con/ You into thinking you're the one . . ." goes the opening couplet, and you can see the flash of recognition in A.J.'s expression, remembering his inarticulate diatribe at the funeral, as if to say, "I wish I could have put it that way." "You kept telling me this guy was good," A.J. says. "It's amazing it was written so long ago. It's like about right now," Rhiannon replies. They soon move closer to each other and begin passionately kissing while Dylan continues coolly venting from the CD player. Rhiannon mounts A.J. and her bra is about to be unhooked, when smoke begins pouring out of the air vent; A.J. made the mistake of parking the car on leaves. But before the car explodes, Dylan's voice can be heard slowing down: *"While one who sings with his tongue on fire . . ."*

"It's Alright, Ma" indeed had legs over forty-two years after its original recording. Twelve days after the *Sopranos* finale, Dylan included it in the set list of his summer tour, which included his return to guitar after he had played only keyboards in concert performance since 2003. In a show I saw at a casino outside Toronto, it was the highlight of the evening. The song had become a slower blues dirge, and Dylan's voice, reduced to a croak, just added drama to a lament that had become the lament of four decades. It surpassed many eras and occasions. Watergate and Clinton impeachment-era crowds had hollered at the line, "Even the president of the United States sometimes must have to stand naked"; Jimmy Carter and Al Gore had invoked the line, "He who is not busy being born is busy dying." And Dylan seemed to be living out the prophecy, doubtlessly continuing to let the song evolve still. Its particular power seemed as mystifying to its author as to anyone else. In a *60 Minutes* segment in 2004, Dylan quoted the song's lyrics to Ed Bradley (who died two years later) as an example of a level of inspiration he could not quite fathom himself: "Try to sit down and write something like that. There's a magic to that, and it's not Siegfried and Roy kind of magic, you know? It's a different kind of a penetrating magic. And, you know, I did it. I did it at one time." When Bradley asked Dylan if he could do it again, Dylan replied: "No . . . You can't do something forever. I did it once, and I can do other things now. But, I can't do that." It was a magic in retrospect, but Dylan was already surveying an exhausted landscape when he wrote "It's Alright Ma." "The Great sayings / have all been said," he wrote in the liner notes to *Bringing It All Back Home.* They are all his, now.

Dylan has, in effect, come to embody the cultural pastiche he wove together so inimitably from "Desolation Row" to "High Water," incongruous elements yoked together. Except that the yoking is less explicit in 2006, when he can assume that bloggers, English teachers, and librarians all across the globe will be scanning his words for attribution. The charges leveled against Dylan would prove ultimately inconsequential for his status as an icon. Dylan has been saying all along that he loves and he thieves, that he's one with Muddy, Cisco, Leadbelly, and all the other magpie hybrids of the

American song he's been sponging for nearly half a century. "Persons attempting to find a motive in this narrative will be prosecuted; persons attempting to find a moral in it will be banished; persons attempting to find a plot in it will be shot." The maxim from Mark Twain at the beginning of *The Adventures of Huckleberry Finn*, a book cribbed for *Chronicles, Vol. 1*, should certainly apply to anything in rock and roll, an art form based on artifice, one that romanticizes the outlaw and banishes the scholar. Anyone with Internet access can be sure that the blogosphere is filled with amateur and professional sleuths creating their own footnotes, tracking down Dylan and his increasingly avaricious muse. In many ways, Dylan's trajectory has been overdetermined. "I was young when I left home," he sang in 1961, a true statement, although he was trying to sound old when he sang it.

"Ain't talkin', just walkin'," he growled on "Ain't Talkin'," the strongest track on *Modern Times* that stood out when the rest of it seemed so enervated, derivative, plagiarized. But it turned out that "Ain't Talkin'" could be the most mind polluting of all—lines and lines lifted from Ovid's *Tristia*. Dylan made other Ovid references on *Modern Times*, too (he says he's been studying "The Art of Love," which he rhymes, somewhat cloyingly, with "fit me like a glove"), but the *Black Sea Letters* and *Tristia*, poems written in exile after the poet was banished by Augustus, resonated most deeply of all. Ovid had been a rock star, perhaps even the voice of his generation in Roman antiquity. But he was also living in a moment of plagiarism—accused of plagiarizing Homer, in a culture that was generally plagiarizing ancient Greece—and, at sixty, in the same age group as the Dylan of *Modern Times*, railed against the unfair forces that cast him away. "Ain't Talkin'," with a total of nine lines taken from *Tristia*, is a great Bob Dylan song anyway. He's at, in the words of Dylan and Peter Green's translation of Ovid, "the last outback at the world's end," intoning lines from Roman antiquity by way of the

Mississippi Delta, Tin Pan Alley, the Confederacy, and God knows what else. "Walkin' with a toothache in my heel," croaks Dylan, a line from "Old Dan Tucker," a minstrel song first published in 1843. No one owns "toothache in my heel." Ovid, Timrod, Bing Crosby are all public domain, the publishing Desolation Row, the dead letter office of song. All textual sources are afloat in a voice that sounds older than his sixty-five years, nearly as ancient as his texts. "In the last outback, at the world's end," Dylan rasps before A-flat minor becomes A-flat major, word for word from Ovid's *Black Sea Letters*. It is a glorious finale, a sublime abyss of stolen fragments and appropriated personae. Dylan never claimed to be exactly who he seemed to be anyway. "It ain't me, babe," he told us, although he is not exactly Bing, Muddy, or Ovid either. In a 1962 interview, he was already making his confession: "Maybe I'm just all these things I soak up. I don't know." In 1965, Dylan sang *about* Desolation Row. In 2006, he made it there, number one with a bullet.

Afterword

"Now You Can Seal Up the Book
and Not Write Anymore"

At some point, Bob Dylan will play his final concert. He will also record his final track, or his final album. And on those final performances, he will still inspire deep feelings of fulfillment, or disappointment, or, though this is less likely, another wave of shock. After this book has closed, the book on Dylan will still be out, although this late in the game, it is increasingly unlikely that he will be decanonized. Even after "Wiggle Wiggle" or "Handy Dandy" (maybe partly *because* of the latter), he will still be welcome at the poet's corner. More awards are likely to follow. "Fame and honor never seem to fade," he groused on *Modern Times*. That was in 2006, pretty late in the game. What was he supposed to be? Gracious? Dylan's fan base is too loyal at this point to abandon ship. Someone who leaves a Dylan concert feeling that the sound mix is off, that the band's musicianship was inconsistent, or that they *could not under-stand a word* has simply failed to see the light. "You think I'm over the hill. You think I'm past my prime?" Dylan will ask in a song, and a boisterous group will yell, on cue, "Noooooo!"

My first Dylan concert was in July 1988, the same month that he performed a stunning version of Leonard Cohen's "Hallelujah" in Cohen's hometown of Montreal, a performance where Dylan's voice veers in all the right directions with a gruff passion. By the time he made it to Dallas a few weeks later, he seemed spent, as if doing a Bob Dylan imitation. I was fifteen and he was forty-seven, which seemed unimaginably old to me at the time. He opened with "Subterranean Homesick Blues," on a tour that included his first live performances of the song. I was too jaded to appreciate that there was something fascinating about how jaded he was. I thought it would be just downhill from there. I didn't realize that it was just the beginning, the first year of the never-ending tour. The next year I bought *Oh Mercy* and practically wore out the vinyl. I realized there could be another chapter, that you could always come back, but not come back all the way. When a friend heard *Time Out of Mind* years later and insisted I get it, I asked, "Is it as good as *Oh Mercy?*" There would be another benchmark.

Eventually, these ups and downs will stop, and latter-day Dylan scholars will have more distance. Part of being a Dylan fan from 1974 onward is the awareness that there is a regular availability of Dylan on stage, but he will not necessarily be the Dylan of your dreams. Dylan keeps moving year after year, and even if you liked him better the year before, you never know what will come next. He has often toured with country musicians older than he is—Merle Haggard, Willie Nelson—perhaps as a reminder that it's possible to be on the road again and again. Dylan's audience has come to resemble the country audience, who are loyal to their stars and allow them to age (unless that star is Dolly Parton). That is, they are like family. They can go gray and long in the tooth and more grizzled in the voice. Dylan has not let himself go gray, but he now sounds older than the hills, with, as he put it, "the blood of the land" in his voice. We are now in the moment of what Edward Said would call Dylan's Late Style. He is now like Yeats's Wild Old Wicked Man, heading to the final mask. We are way past expecting him to stay forever young. We now want him to be forever human, forever visceral. It turns out that it is not always better to burn out than to fade away. Dylan's fade is poignant, as subtle and haunting as a late Rembrandt self-portrait. "Even if the flesh falls off of my face, I know someone will be there to care." We don't know who exactly he was singing about, if it was anyone particular. What we do know is that the curtain will close, the recording will stop, but someone will be there to care. New volumes of the *Bootleg Series* will be issued. New courses will be taught, new books will be written, a new audience will see the light. We will walk down another road.

Appendix

PLAYLIST, O PLAYLIST

As a guide to the perplexed (or to the familiar), in celebration of Bob Dylan's seventieth birthday, I have assembled a list of seventy essential Dylan tracks. Considering that Dylan has written more than 500 songs, the idea might seem severe, even monstrous. Chiseling down half a century of work to as many tracks as Dylan has years, this venture has forced me to, when up against the wall, name seventy tracks I would not want to do without, even if it means sacrificing some of my fondlings. In a different mood, I might have sacrificed slightly differently, but I would have to say that the tracks below represent Dylan at his zenith, and the variety among them should give a good representation of every period worth representing. I can only greet with sadness that Generation Download has lost what I regard as that great and now nearly extinct art form: the long-playing record album. It is hard for me to think of Dylan's songs without the sequencing of *Freewheelin'* or *Bringing It All Back Home* (I will always think "acoustic side" and "electric side"), *Highway 61 Revisited*, *Blonde on Blonde* (again, always with the "Sad Eyed

Lady" side), and so on. But I must acknowledge that downloading also means easy and ready accessibility. Hence this list: threescore years and ten of as good as Dylan gave, in alphabetical order.

When an alternate or live track is truly illuminating, I put it in parentheses, but the first version listed is the definitive one, at least according to this highly idiosyncratic Baedeker. (And I acknowledge that choosing between a *Basement Tapes* version and a 1971 session can be a mug's game.) I considered adding cover versions, but then I realized that I would just keep telling people they should listen to Jimi Hendrix and Nina Simone, as if they didn't know that already. And if I had one duet with Joan Baez, then I would have to have a lopsided amount, so there are no duets with anyone, just background harmonies by Emmylou Harris or members of The Band, among others. Also, I happen to have a preference for the original New York sessions for *Blood on the Tracks*, as opposed to the Minnesota sessions, which I still love, and which I grew up on, but which, to my ears, gild the lily, so the list reflects that. (The issued album is a hybrid.) If it's a scandal for some to supersede *The Bootleg Series, Vol. 1* for *Blood on the Tracks*, I will simply let my own predilections stand (in this case for lower registers and subtler emotions) and let a thousand flowers bloom. Also, I did include a few bootlegs, but I tried to do so sparingly, since the idea is to direct listeners to something easily accessible and street legal, so to speak. There are some songs that I discuss at length in the book that are not on this list, which demonstrates something about the distinction among narrative, argument, and hierarchy. I have also left off some personal favorites in favor of what is more obviously important. The most popular Dylan songs neglected here are "Rainy Day Women #12 and 35" (a live performance made me like the song more after years of skipping to track 2 on *Blonde on Blonde*) and "Knockin' on Heaven's Door" (which I like, but which simply has less to it than the songs listed here, which might be part of its magic, but oh well). Some less popular that I eliminated with a heavy heart included "Brownsville Girl," "Tough Mama," "Hazel," "I Threw It All Away," "Pledging My Time," "To Ramona," "Spanish Harlem Incident," "I and I," "Too Much of Nothin'," "Dignity," and "You're a Big Girl Now," and this final track eventually had to go or I was in danger of listing all of *Blood on the Tracks*. And I hope Sony eventually issues the live version of "Abandoned Love," one of the most theatrical and emotionally raw Dylan performances ever committed to low-fi audio, superior to the studio outtake on *Biograph*. I also hope for *Blood on the Tracks* and *Infidels* variora, and I expect them to be unearthed. Also, again to narrow it down, there are no covers. (There are a few collaborations, all acknowledged.) Diehard Dylanites will surely be scandalized by some omission or other. When he turns 100, I'll make a longer list.

Seventy on Seventy

1. A Hard Rain's A-Gonna Fall
   Freewheelin' Bob Dylan (Live 1975)
2. Abandoned Love
   Golden Unplugged Album (Biograph)
3. Ain't Talkin' Modern Times (Tell Tale Signs)
4. All Along the Watchtower
   John Wesley Harding (Before the Flood)
5. Ballad of a Thin Man
   Highway 61 Revisited (Live 1966)
6. Blind Willie McTell
   Bootleg Series, Vol. 1 (Outfidel Intakes)
7. Blowin' in the Wind
   Freewheelin' Bob Dylan
8. Crash on the Levee (Down in the Flood)
   Greatest Hits Vol. 2 (Genuine Basement Tapes)

9. Desolation Row
   Highway 61 Revisited (No Direction Home Soundtrack)
10. Don't Think Twice, It's Alright
    Freewheelin' Bob Dylan
11. Every Grain of Sand
    Shot of Love (Bootleg Series)
12. Forever Young
    Planet Waves (Biograph, The Last Waltz)
13. Gates of Eden
    Bringing It All Back Home
14. Girl from the North Country
    Freewheelin' Bob Dylan (Nashville Skyline)
15. Groom's Still Waiting at the Altar
    Shot of Love
16. High Water (For Charley Patton)
    "Love and Theft"
17. I Shall Be Released
    Greatest Hits, Vol. 2 (Bootleg Series)
18. I Want You
    Blonde on Blonde
19. Idiot Wind
    Bootleg Series (Blood on the Tracks, Hard Rain)
20. Isis (with Jacques Levy)
    Desire (Biograph)
21. It Ain't Me, Babe
    Another Side of Bob Dylan
22. It Takes a Lot to Laugh, It Takes a Train to Cry
    Highway 61 Revisited
23. It's All Over Now, Baby Blue
    Bringing It All Back Home
24. It's Alright, Ma (I'm Only Bleeding)
    Bringing It All Back Home

25. Jokerman
   Infidels (Letterman rehearsal and performance)
26. Just Like a Woman
   Blonde on Blonde (Live 1966)
27. Just Like Tom Thumb's Blues
   Highway 61 Revisited (Live, 1966)
28. Lay, Lady, Lay
   Nashville Skyline
29. Like a Rolling Stone
   Highway 61 Revisited (Bootleg Series; Live, 1966; Self Portrait)
30. Love Minus Zero/No Limit
   Bringing It All Back Home
31. Maggie's Farm
   Bringing It All Back Home
32. Mama, You Been on My Mind
   Bootleg Series, Vol. 1
33. Man in the Long Black Coat
   Oh Mercy
34. Masters of War
   Freewheelin' Bob Dylan
35. Mississippi
   "Love and Theft" (all three versions on Tell Tale Signs)
36. Most of the Time
   Oh Mercy
37. Mr. Tambourine Man
   Bringing It All Back Home
38. My Back Pages
   Another Side of Bob Dylan
39. Not Dark Yet
   Time Out of Mind
40. Obviously Five Believers
   Blonde on Blonde

41. Odds and Ends
    The Basement Tapes (The Genuine Basement Tapes)
42. One More Cup of Coffee (Valley Below)
    Desire
43. One Too Many Mornings
    The Times They Are a-Changin' (Live, 1966; Dylan-Cash sessions)
44. Percy's Song
    Biograph
45. Positively Fourth Street
    Greatest Hits
46. Quinn the Eskimo (Mighty Quinn)
    Self-Portrait (Biograph, Genuine Basement Tapes)
47. Sad-Eyed Lady of the Lowlands
    Blonde on Blonde
48. Sara
    Desire (Live 1975)
49. She Belongs to Me
    Bringing It All Back Home (Self Portrait)
50. Shelter from the Storm
    Blood on the Tracks (Hard Rain)
51. Simple Twist of Fate
    Blood on the Tracks (Live 1975)
52. Standing in the Doorway
    Time Out of Mind
53. Subterranean Homesick Blues
    Bringing It All Back Home (Bootleg Series)
54. Stuck Inside of Mobile with the Memphis Blues Again
    Blonde on Blonde
55. Sweetheart Like You
    Infidels (Outfidel Intakes, Rough Cuts)

56. Tangled Up in Blue
    Bootleg Series (Blood on the Tracks, Real Live)
57. Tears of Rage (with Richard Manuel)
    The Basement Tapes (Genuine Basement Tapes)
58. The Lonesome Death of Hattie Carroll
    The Times They Are a-Changin (Live 1975)
59. The Times They Are a-Changin'
    The Times They Are a-Changin'
60. Things Have Changed
    The Essential Bob Dylan
61. This Wheel's on Fire
    Basement Tapes (Genuine Basement Tapes)
62. Tonight I'll Be Staying Here with You
    Nashville Skyline (Live 1975)
63. Tryin' to Get to Heaven
    Time Out of Mind
64. Up to Me
    Biograph
65. Visions of Johanna
    Blonde on Blonde (Biograph)
66. When I Paint My Masterpiece
    Greatest Hits, Vol. 2
67. Where Are You Tonight? (Journey Through Dark Heat)
    Street Legal
68. Where Teardrops Fall
    Oh Mercy
69. You Ain't Goin' Nowhere
    Greatest Hits Vol. 2 (Basement Tapes, Genuine Basement Tapes)
70. You're Gonna Make Me Lonesome When You Go
    Blood on the Tracks

Notes

Epigraph, p. viii: from "Tangled Up in Blue"

ONE

The Cawing, Derisive Voice

1. Quote from the *Daily Telegraph*, November 10, 1965.
2. There have been exceptions, of course, including Paula West's "Like a Rolling Stone," Bill Frisell's "Just Like a Woman," and Nina Simone's "Just Like Tom Thumb's Blues."
3. Mary Colruso, "A Taste of 'Honey': Lucinda Williams Dishes on Her Art and Album of Bittersweet Tunes," *Birmingham News*, February 27, 2009.
4. Bowie's quote can be found in Ira Nadel, *Various Positions: A Life of Leonard Cohen*. New York: Vintage, 1996.
5. This is a song title by Elvis Costello that first appeared on his *King of America* (CBS/Columbia, 1986).
6. For more on how the best of *Infidels* was left on the cutting room floor, see Jonathan Lethem in *The Cambridge Companion to Bob Dylan*: "Perhaps I've persuaded you (I hope I have) that Infidels doesn't exist. It's a kit: construct your own. Surely there's a version you'll award four stars" (166). Lethem speaks for many, including biographers Clinton Heylin and Howard Sounes, who corroborate from the discarded tapes that, on *Infidels*, the unheard melodies were indeed sweeter.

7. See Robert Polito, "Bob Dylan's Memory Palace," *Highway 61 Revisited: Bob Dylan's Road from Minnesota to the World*, ed. Colleen J. Sheehy and Thomas Swiss (Minneapolis: University of Minnesota Press, 2009).
8. See Sadi Ranson-Polizzotti, "Simon Cowell on Bob Dylan: Boring," http://blogcritics.org/music/article/simon-cowell-on-bob-dylan-boring.

TWO

Screen Test

1. Quoted in "Docufictions: An Interview with Martin Scorsese on Documentary Film," *Film History* 19, no. 2 (2007).

THREE

Not Dark Yet

1. "Must Be Santa," a polka number from *Christmas in the Heart* (2009), was, along with "Talking Hava Negiliah Blues" (1963), as close as he is likely to come.
2. Monk may have been intentionally echoing a statement made by Louis Armstrong: "All music is folk music." Cited in "Louis Armstrong, Jazz Trumpeter and Singer, Dies," *New York Times*, July 7, 1971.
3. Wilson would eventually be replaced by Bob Johnston.
4. This is available on the Mexican DVD *Bob Dylan: Hard to Handle (with Tom Petty and the Heartbreakers)*, originally broadcast on HBO.
5. "Bob Dylan on Barack Obama, Ulysses Grant and American Civil War Ghosts," Bill Flanagan, Times Online UK, April 6, 2009.

FOUR

Don't Steal, Don't Lift

1. John Keats, *Letters*, Vol. 2, G. P. Putnam, 1848.
2. Some of these appropriations were first spotted in a blog called *Ralph the Sacred River* (*ralphriver.blogspot.com*) run by Edward Cook.
3. Dylan must have gotten the message when he released *Together Through Life* (2009), in which "My Wife's Hometown," which uses the melody of "I Just Want to Make Love to You," shares the credit with the estate of Willie Dixon.
4. Dylan would break his own record, hitting number one three years later (and older) with *Together Through Life* (2009).
5. Few knew it at the time, but Dylan had a four-year-old daughter, Desiree Gabrielle, the "Gabby Goo Goo" who is the dedicatee of the album, which

is filled with nursery rhymes. This at least explains such verse, done more convincingly elsewhere on the album.

6. Another unreleased track from those sessions, "Red River Shore," was finally unearthed on *Tell Tale Signs (The Bootleg Series, Vol. 8)* (2009), a song more wistful than lovesick. The three versions of "Mississippi" show Dylan in conflict with Lanois's atmospheric approach. After a gorgeous demo, one studio version is too smooth, another, with altered lyrics, works against itself too perversely.

Selected Bibliography

Adorno, Theodor, "On Lyric Poetry and Society," in *Notes to Literature*, trans. Shierry Weber Nicholsen. New York: Columbia University Press, 1991.

Bob Dylan: Dont Look Back (1965 Tour Deluxe Edition). Directed by D. A. Pennebaker. New Video Group, 2007. DVD, 152 min.

Bowden, Betsy. *Performed Literature: Words and Music by Bob Dylan*. 2nd ed. Lanham: University Press of America, 2001.

Christie, Ian, and David Thompson, eds. *Scorsese on Scorsese*, rev. ed. London: Faber and Faber, 2003.

Cott, Jonathan, ed. *Bob Dylan: The Essential Interviews*. New York: Wenner Books, 2006.

Dettmar, Kevin J. H., ed. *The Cambridge Companion to Bob Dylan*. Cambridge: Cambridge University Press, 2009.

Dickstein, Morris. *Gates of Eden: American Culture in the Sixties*. New York: Basic Books, 1977.

Donato, Raffaele. "Docufictions: An Interview with Martin Scorsese on Documentary Film." *Film History* 19, no. 2 (2007).

Dylan, Bob. *Tarantula.* New York: St. Martin's, 1994.

———. *Chronicles: Vol. 1.* New York: Simon & Schuster, 2004.

F for Fake. Directed by Orson Welles. Criterion Collection, 2005. DVD, 89 min.

Gates, David. "The Book of Bob." *Newsweek,* October 4, 2004.

Ginsberg, Allen. *Collected Poems, 1947–1997.* New York: Harper-Collins, 2007.

Hajdu, David. *Positively 4th Street: The Lives and Times of Joan Baez, Bob Dylan, Mimi Baez-Farina and Richard Farina.* New York: Farrar, Straus and Giroux, 2001.

Hedin, Benjamin. *Studio A: The Bob Dylan Reader.* New York: W. W Norton & Co., 2004.

Heylin, Clinton. *Bob Dylan: Behind the Shades Revisited.* New York: HarperCollins, 2001.

Hoberman, J. "Like a Complete Unknown: *I'm Not There* and the Changing Face of Bob Dylan on Film." *The Village Voice,* November 13, 2007.

Histoire(s) du cinema. Directed by Jean-Luc Godard. Three-disc set, import, PAL, subtitled. Gaumont, 1988–98. DVD, 265 min.

I'm Not There. Two-disc collector's edition. Directed by Todd Haynes. Screenplay by Todd Haynes and Oren Moverman. Weinstein Company, 2007. DVD, 135 min.

Koestenbaum, Wayne. *Andy Warhol.* New York: Lipper/Viking, 2001.

The Last Waltz. Special Edition. Directed by Martin Scorsese. MGM, 2002. DVD, 117 min.

Lethem, Jonathan. "The Genius of Bob Dylan." *Rolling Stone,* September 6, 2006.

"Life Lessons" from *New York Stories.* Directed by Martin Scorsese. Screenplay by Richard Price. Touchstone Pictures, 2003. DVD, 124 min.

Lott, Eric. *Love and Theft: Blackface Minstrelsy and the American Working Class.* New York: Oxford, 1993.

Mailer, Norman. *The Executioner's Song*. New York: Vintage, 1998.

Marcus, Greil. *The Old, Weird America: The World of Bob Dylan's Basement Tapes*. New York: Picador, 1997.

———. *Like a Rolling Stone: Bob Dylan at the Crossroads*. New York: Public Affairs, 2005.

———. *Bob Dylan: Writings, 1968–2010*. New York: Public Affairs, 2010.

Marqusee, Mike. *Wicked Messenger: Bob Dylan and the 1960s*. New York: Seven Stories Press, 2005.

Masked and Anonymous. Directed by Larry Charles. Columbia Tristar, 2004. DVD.

Morrison, James. *The Cinema of Todd Haynes: All That Heaven Allows*. London: Wallflower Press, 2007.

Negus, Keith. *Bob Dylan*. Bloomington: Indiana University Press, 2008.

No Direction Home. Directed by Martin Scorsese. Paramount Home Video, 2005. DVD, 208 min.

The Other Side of the Mirror: Bob Dylan Live at the Newport Folk Festival, 1963–1965. Sony, 2007. DVD, 83 min.

Ovid. *The Poems of Exile: Tristia and the Black Sea Letters*. Trans. Peter Green. Berkeley: University of California Press, 2005.

Polizzotti, Mark. *Highway 61 Revisited (33 1/3)*. New York: Continuum, 2006.

Proust, Marcel. *In Search of Lost Time*. Trans. C. K. Scott Moncrieff, Terence Kilmartin, and D. J. Enright. New York: Modern Library, 2003.

Ricks, Christopher. *Dylan's Visions of Sin*. New York: Ecco, 2003.

Rogovy, Seth. *Bob Dylan: Prophet, Mystic Poet*. New York: Scribner, 2010.

Safe. Directed by Todd Haynes. Sony Pictures, 2001. DVD, 119 min.

Sheehy, Colleen J., and Thomas Swiss, eds. *Highway 61 Revisited: Bob Dylan's Road from Minnesota to the World*. Minneapolis: University of Minnesota Press, 2009.

Shelton, Robert. *No Direction Home: The Life and Music of Bob Dylan.* New York: William Morrow & Co., 1986.

Sloman, Larry. "Ratso." *On the Road With Bob Dylan.* New York: Bantam, 1978.

Sounes, Howard. *Down the Highway: The Life of Bob Dylan.* New York: Grove Press, 2001.

Spitz, Bob. *Bob Dylan: A Biography.* New York: McGraw-Hill, 1989.

Sullivan, Robert. "This Is Not a Bob Dylan Movie." *New York Times Magazine*, October 7, 2007.

Timrod, Henry. *The Collected Poems of Henry Timrod: A Variorum Edition.* Athens: University of Georgia Press, 2007.

Velvet Goldmine. Directed by Todd Haynes; screenplay by Todd Haynes; story by Todd Haynes and James Lyons. Miramax, 1998. DVD, 124 min.

Warhol, Andy. "Screen Test: Bob Dylan," 1965. 16mm film, black and white, one minute. Collection of The Andy Warhol Museum, Pittsburgh.

Wilentz, Sean. *Bob Dylan in America.* New York: Doubleday, 2010.

Credits

Bob Dylan's Blues

Brownsville Girl

Changing of the Guards

Chimes of Freedom

Desolation Row

Don't Think Twice, It's Alright

Forever Young

From A Buick 6

George Jackson

Sad Eyed Lady of the Lowlands
Copyright © 1966 by Dwarf Music; renewed 1994 by Dwarf Music. All rights reserved. International copyright secured. Reprinted by permission.

Sara
Copyright © 1975, 1976 by Ram's Horn Music; renewed 2003, 2004 by Ram's Horn Music. All rights reserved. International copyright secured. Reprinted by permission.

Slow Train
Copyright © 1979 by Special Rider Music. All rights reserved. International copyright secured. Reprinted by permission.

Song to Woody
Copyright © 1962, 1965 by Duchess Music Corporation; renewed 1990, 1993 by MCA. All rights reserved. International copyright secured. Reprinted by permission.

Spanish Harlem Incident
Copyright © 1964 by Warner Bros. Inc.; renewed 1992 by Special Rider Music. All rights reserved. International copyright secured. Reprinted by permission.

Standing in the Doorway
Copyright © 1997 by Special Rider Music. All rights reserved. International copyright secured. Reprinted by permission.

Subterranean Homesick Blues
Copyright © 1965 by Warner Bros. Inc.; renewed 1993 by Special Rider Music. All rights reserved. International copyright secured. Reprinted by permission.

Sugar Baby
Copyright © 2001 by Special Rider Music. All rights reserved. International copyright secured. Reprinted by permission.

Summer Days
Copyright © 2001 by Special Rider Music. All rights reserved. International copyright secured. Reprinted by permission.

Sweetheart Like You
Copyright © 1983 by Special Rider Music. All rights reserved. International copyright secured. Reprinted by permission.

Index

All music is by Bob Dylan unless otherwise indicated.

153

Spivey, Victoria, 80, 89
Springs, Helena, 79, 81
Springsteen, Bruce, 4, 30, 95
"St. James Infirmary Blues," 85
"Stage Fright" (Robertson), 15, 64
"Standing in the Doorway," 113, 134
Stanton, Harry Dean, 109
Staple Singers, 75
Staples, Mavis, 74–75, 86–87
Starr, Ringo, 39
"Steel Bars" (Bolton and Dylan), 105–6
Stein, Gertrude, 107
Steinbeck, John, 67, 109
Steve Allen Show, 43, 96, 110
Stewart, Potter, 85
Sting, 52
Stone, Ron, 37
Street-Legal, 22, 23, 39, 78–81
"Stuck Inside of Mobile with the Memphis Blues Again," 46, 134
"Subterranean Homesick Blues," 4, 94–96, 120, 126, 134
"Sugar Baby," 119
"Summer Days," 119
Sun Ra, 71
Sun Records, 115
Superstar: The Karen Carpenter Story, 46
Surrealism, 74, 80
"Sweetheart Like You," 24, 100–101, 134

"Taking It Easy" (Seeger), 95
"Talking Hava Negiliah Blues," 138*n*1
"Talking John Birch Paranoid Blues," 10
"Tangled Up in Blue," 50, 135
Tarantula (Dylan), 47, 75–77, 97
Taxi Driver, 33, 35, 36
Taylor, Cecil, 62, 71
"Tears of Rage," 14, 135
Tell Tale Signs, 139*n*6
Terrorist attacks, 115–16
"Things Have Changed," 28–29, 115, 135
"This Wheel's on Fire," 135
"Thunder on the Mountain," 87
Thurmond, Strom, 117
Till, Emmett, 67
Till, Paul, 50
Timberlake, Justin, 101
Time, Love, and Tenderness (Bolton), 105–6
Time magazine, 19
Time Out of Mind, 28, 104, 112–16, 126
The Times They Are a-Changin', 5, 6–7
"The Times They Are a-Changin'," 75, 91, 115, 135
Timrod, Henry, 101, 124
Tin Pan Alley songwriters, 2–3, 5, 100
"To Ramona," 70, 131
Together Through Life, 29, 51, 138*nn*3–4